Cambridge

Elements in Reinventing Capitalism
edited by
Arie Y. Lewin
Duke University
Till Talaulicar
University of Erfurt

ABERRANT CAPITALISM

The Decay and Revival of Customer Capitalism

Hunter Hastings
Bialla Venture Partners and Kingman Institute

Stephen Denning
SD Learning Consortium

CAMBRIDGE
UNIVERSITY PRESS

Shaftesbury Road, Cambridge CB2 8EA, United Kingdom

One Liberty Plaza, 20th Floor, New York, NY 10006, USA

477 Williamstown Road, Port Melbourne, VIC 3207, Australia

314–321, 3rd Floor, Plot 3, Splendor Forum, Jasola District Centre,
New Delhi – 110025, India

103 Penang Road, #05–06/07, Visioncrest Commercial, Singapore 238467

Cambridge University Press is part of Cambridge University Press & Assessment,
a department of the University of Cambridge.

We share the University's mission to contribute to society through the pursuit of
education, learning and research at the highest international levels of excellence.

www.cambridge.org
Information on this title: www.cambridge.org/9781009478793

DOI: 10.1017/9781009348867

First published 2024

A catalogue record for this publication is available from the British Library.

ISBN 978-1-009-47879-3 Hardback
ISBN 978-1-009-34882-9 Paperback
ISSN 2634-8950 (online)
ISSN 2634-8942 (print)

Aberrant Capitalism

The Decay and Revival of Customer Capitalism

Elements in Reinventing Capitalism

DOI: 10.1017/9781009348867
First published online: February 2024

Hunter Hastings
Bialla Venture Partners and Kingman Institute

Stephen Denning
SD Learning Consortium

Author for correspondence: Hunter Hastings, hunterhastings@icloud.com

Abstract: The corporation was a timely emergent phenomenon of the capitalist system. Under entrepreneurial ownership with customer value creation goals, corporations introduced new products and services, new capital structures and new management processes capable of improving customer experiences in every facet of their lives. After entrepreneurship, the organizational model transitioned to managerial capitalism, and from there into command-and-control and central planning. Then came further transition into the era of financialization, where shareholder value replaced customer value as the purpose of the corporation. Managers diverted resources to their own enrichment as well as that of shareholders, at the expense of investment in future innovation. Capitalism's reputation has become tarnished and its purpose distorted. This Element ends with the promise of another emergent era, via the corporations of the digital age.

This Element also has a video abstract: www.Cambridge.org/Hastings

Keywords: entrepreneurial management, corporate capitalism, financialization, customer capitalism, value creation

ISBNs: 9781009478793 (HB), 9781009348829 (PB), 9781009348867 (OC)
ISSNs: 2634-8950 (online), 2634-8942 (print)

Contents

Those who confuse entrepreneurship and management close their eyes to the economic problem. The capitalist system is not a managerial system; it is an entrepreneurial system.

Ludwig von Mises (Mises, Human Action 1998)

1 Introduction

Capitalism is the economic system associated with the greatest increase in human well-being in all of history. Many observers have used per capita income as the proxy for human well-being and depicted its increase graphically to give it a special impact. Gregory Clark in *Farewell to Alms: A Brief Economic History of the World* (Clark, 2007), describes a significant break in real income per capita around 1800, the beginning of the Industrial Revolution (see Figure 1).

Despite this historical record, capitalism as an economic system is viewed with skepticism and attracts much criticism, often bitter and passionate. The primary criticisms can be grouped as follows:

- Income inequality: Critics argue that capitalism tends to exacerbate income inequality; some members of society are paid well while others are not, and some view the disparities as extreme and unjustifiable.
- Wealth inequality: Capitalism is viewed as rewarding individuals and businesses based on their ability to generate wealth for themselves (as opposed to value for others). This can lead to a concentration of wealth in the hands of a few while a large portion of the population struggles to generate any wealth at all. Critics contend that this unequal distribution of wealth can limit social mobility and contribute to societal unrest.
- Exploitation of labor: Some argue that capitalism incentivizes businesses to maximize profits by minimizing labor costs, which can result in exploitation. This might manifest in the form of low wages, inadequate working conditions, or even the use of child labor. Critics assert that this exploitation can perpetuate a cycle of poverty for workers and their families.
- Environmental degradation: Critics argue that capitalism's emphasis on growth and profit can lead to a focus on short-term gains at the expense of long-term environmental sustainability. Critics argue that the drive for profits can result in overconsumption of resources, pollution, and other forms of environmental harm, which can have long-lasting negative effects on the planet and future generations, and that the capitalist system will always resist the adjustments necessary for the avoidance of climate disaster.

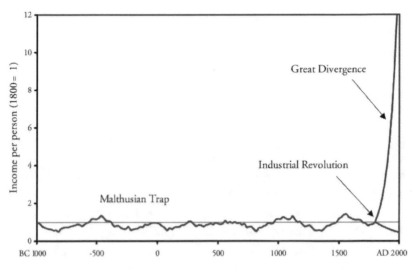

Figure 1 World economic history at a glance. Income levels rose sharply in many countries after 1800. Reproduced from Gregory Clark's A *Farewell to Alms: A Brief Economic History of the World*

- Boom and bust cycles: Critics point out that capitalism is prone to economic cycles of growth and recession, often referred to as "boom and bust" cycles. These fluctuations can lead to periods of high unemployment, financial instability, and reduced economic growth. Some argue that these cycles are inherent to capitalism and that the system lacks the ability to effectively address or prevent them.
- Erosion of social welfare: Lastly, some critics argue that the competitive nature of capitalism can undermine social welfare and public services and reduce access for vulnerable populations. Additionally, critics contend that the focus on individual wealth accumulation can erode social cohesion and the sense of collective responsibility. Some go so far as to say that the materialism fostered by capitalism erodes morality and undermines religion.

In the current age, many of these criticisms pertain more to corporations and their management than to the underlying concepts of the capitalist system itself. It is corporations that generate income in the form of wages; it is corporations that generate wealth by enhancing the value of financial and other kinds of assets; it is corporations that harness labor to their purposes; it is corporations who consume input resources and output polluting waste; it is corporations who make the errors that constitute economic busts as well as the successes that constitute booms; and it is corporations who could be accused of ignoring the populations that are not their employees, suppliers, or customers.

We present the case that these criticisms are largely misplaced. One of the purposes of *The Elements in Reinventing Capitalism* series is to investigate the context of these misplaced criticisms. Herein, we find other criticisms that are more pertinent as opportunities for improvement.

Corporations: The Primary Protagonists of Capitalism

Corporations have been the primary protagonists of capitalism since the middle of the 1800s. Corporations bent the curve of economic progress and achieved the continuous increase in GDP per capita illustrated in Clark's chart. Yet, today, the corporation attracts additional emotional criticisms beyond the critique of the system. Corporations are often seen as cold, heartless, cynical, untrustworthy, and soulless, with dark motivations and evil intent. These are emotional critiques, and we can move beyond them to a more systemic view.

Corporations are a brilliant innovation within the system of capitalism, emerging unexpectedly from the human interactions within the complex adaptive system we can call "the economy". Complex adaptive systems (CAS) are typically described as comprising agents – individuals, companies, departments, governments, and institutions – who interact and influence each other's behaviors and decisions, resulting in feedback loops from which learning, adaptation and dynamic change can come. Emergence is the description of outcomes that cannot be predicted from the behavior of the individual agents or be causally attributed.

The corporations we pay attention to in this Element emerged in a peculiar form in the middle of the nineteenth century and have continued to evolve. They have become a predominant focus of modern economic life and the primary means of organizing that life. The modern business corporation combines the potential for perpetual succession, a separate legal personality, centralized management, shared ownership of capital, transferable shares and limited liability (Rona, 2017). Later in its evolution, the corporation integrated these features with the tools of mathematical economics so as to operate with analytical managerial discipline. When this analytical discipline became focused on the continuous maximization of share price, rather than on human betterment, some corporations assumed an artificial purpose that came to be seen by their managers as an exemption from human and ethical responsibilities.

Another feature of complex adaptive systems to draw on in order to understand the dynamics of the evolution of the corporation is entropy. All systems exhibit entropy, defined as a loss of energy (or, more strictly, a loss of the availability of some energy to do work). Here we employ the term metaphorically, as Lazare Carnot originally formulated it: lost useful work (Persch, 2020).

In corporations, early-stage entropic trends were exhibited in waste, pollution, and bureaucracy. There was more entropy to come: inattentiveness to customers, neglect of employees, and reduced responsiveness to the need for change signaled by feedback loops, slower and less impactful innovation, increased levels of command-and-control management, and the processes of financialization that squeezed out investment in the innovative improvement of production. Entropy can bring about the death of systems. Corporations that have succumbed to these trends can be thought of as aberrations of capitalism.

Happily, in the case of open systems, where new energy can enter exogenously from an external source, new islands of excellence can establish themselves and grow, even though they must exist and find ways to thrive alongside the entropic debris of the old system. We see signs of this renewal in the new corporations of the digital era. The new energy enters mostly via the new internet-based business models that give greater direct control to customers through networks, enabling a bottom-up and outside-in dynamic that leads to a completely different organizational approach from the top-down, hierarchical, multi-divisional forms of the preceding corporate structures. The rate of evolutionary change promises to be rapid.

The Organization of This Element

This element starts with a brief overview of capitalism before the corporation and explores some of its features. We then illustrate the enormous economic and social impact of new corporate forms of the second half of the nineteenth century through the rapid rise of the (primarily) US corporations, which became known collectively as big business. Rather than characterizing their founders as "robber barons," we highlight their economic function as owner-entrepreneurs, innovating a model of economic organization that was very different from anything that had gone before and, in hindsight, equally different than the models of managerial capitalism that evolved afterwards.

We trace the evolution of the corporation through the exit of the owner-entrepreneurs and the changing forms and styles of management, including new discoveries in the areas of both effectiveness (capacity to serve customers and meet their needs) and efficiency (reduced costs for doing so). We identify pivotal changes as the twentieth century proceeds, especially the gradual embrace of command-and-control methods of management, and the increasing cultural commitment to central planning, all of which were exacerbated by the experiences of wartime economies. The end of the twentieth century brought more entropic influences in the form of financialization and rampant bureaucracy.

Throughout, the evolution of technology exerts an independent influence, as the principal exogenous factor. In the nineteenth century, new technologies spurred the second industrial revolution of mass production and mass distribution. The owner-entrepreneurs invented management to harness the economic power inherent in these new technologies. From then on, electricity, railroads, oil, the internal combustion engine, steel, chemicals, and eventually computers, telecommunications and the internet, and all the other evolved and evolving technologies required an ever-changing organizing response from corporations. The parallel paths of technological and corporate evolution continue their advance toward an unknown and unpredictable future.

2 Capitalism Before Corporations

Adam Smith is cited as the author of the "founding text of modern capitalism" (Kristol, 1995), but we must go back one generation to Richard Cantillon, who, in his text, *An Essay on Economic Theory, 1730*, was the first to describe an enterprise economy in the details of its operation. He provided the first extended study of the organization of commercial society based on what he christened "entrepreneurs" (Cantillon, 2010). Cantillon also unleashed the market economy and generated great prosperity. The entrepreneurs established markets in villages and towns, where they bought and sold goods and established prices, and made profits. There were greater numbers of entrepreneurs in cities with a larger and wealthier population. They were the prime directors of resources. Typically, they generated enough cash flow to acquire their own capital without borrowing.

They were merchants, builders, restauranteurs, innkeepers, providers of transport, carpenters, retailers and many other kinds of artisans and tradespeople, and, of course, were close to their customers, competing on specialization, quality, convenience and price to retain those customers. They recognized that "their customers may leave them any day."

Adam Smith was familiar with Cantillon's work, and in his *Inquiry into the Nature and Causes of the Wealth of Nations*, used the English translation "undertaker" to describe the entrepreneurial role, as well as the term "projector" for those who "attempt to establish a new manufacture" in order to make (sometimes) extraordinary profits. He was aware that the customer-centricity of small businesses and artisans provided discipline. "Finding their profits to rise by the favor of their customers, (they) increase as much as possible their skill and industry." The idea was to have "a hundred or a thousand" different customers – obliged to them all but not absolutely dependent on any one of them.

Thus, it is fair to say that Smith had a concept of customer capitalism insofar as he recognized that serving and pleasing customers was the determinant of business success, stability, and longevity. Customers could be aristocrats (or princes, as Smith often referred to them) or, more often, their agents, or they could be fellow artisans, farmers, and local service providers (the butcher, the brewer, and the baker). They were, for the most part, close by, and most trade was face to face.

After Smith, the size distribution of companies became more variable, with a large number of small and medium-sized enterprises operating alongside a very small number of large corporations. Merchants were the business leaders in pre-industrial Great Britain, serving as lynchpins holding together local and regional economies. Industrialization took place in Great Britain earlier than in America, but local, regional and family businesses continued to be more the norm than big businesses. The majority of businesses were family owned and operated, and most of them operated in local or regional markets. Businesses were generally organized as partnerships, with individual owners or family members taking on specific roles and responsibilities within the company. There were a few joint stock companies that pooled investor capital in return for a share of the profits in the enterprise. There was a particular emphasis on textiles, iron and steel and transportation. Delivering quality products at a competitive price was the driver of success. Many businesses relied on personal relationships with customers, with owners and managers often interacting directly with clients and developing long-term relationships with them. Nevertheless, the competitive environment of the period did incentivize businesses to pay attention to customer preferences and demands. It was well-established that the businesses which demonstrated the ability to respond to fast-changing customer needs and desires were more likely to succeed in the marketplace (Blackford, n.d.).

Wedgwood & Bentley

Wedgwood & Bentley can be considered a representative firm of this period. It was a partnership between Josiah Wedgwood, a potter, and Thomas Bentley, a merchant and entrepreneur. The partnership developed a new and innovative product, creamware, which offered a better appearance than the mass market pottery of the time, with an attractive white surface, and a "rich and brilliant glaze" that was durable under hot and cold temperatures (for the newly fashionable hot beverages such as tea, coffee, and hot chocolate), with a simplified lower-cost manufacturing process that enabled lower consumer pricing. Consumer tastes were changing, and novel products of higher quality generated high demand across a broadening market.

Wedgwood & Bentley adopted new, technologically innovative manufacturing infrastructure, including engine-turned lathes and coal ovens, and new volume production techniques. They used novel raw materials, new casting processes, distinctive molds, and new firing methods to increase the quality, quantity and range of output. Josiah Wedgwood compiled "Experiment Books" to codify precise, systematic knowledge of production techniques. The partnership invested in training for their workforce, and in detailed process manuals and novel organizational designs. They utilized (and invested in) the new infrastructure of canals to ship their products to new markets.

They further segmented their consumer market by identifying a luxury segment (differentiated from "useful ware") among the aristocracy and royalty of Europe. The Wedgwood 50-person dinner service of 952 pieces, each one painted with a distinctive British scene, designed for Catherine The Great of Russia, was displayed in London as a marketing event before being shipped to the empress's court. Wedgwood & Bentley understood that marketing was as important as manufacturing, and established display showrooms in multiple cities. They regularly sent unsolicited parcels of pottery to members of the aristocracy and nobility, along with an invoice, and the alternative of free return shipping. The marketing technique was successful and profitable. The firm practiced active brand marketing, firing the Wedgwood name onto every piece. Another new line was Queensware, after the production of a tea set for King George III's wife resulted in the firm being appointed as "Potter To her Majesty." They understood celebrity endorsement just as well as Nike does today, and were astutely aware that middle class customers aspired to the same brands as the court and nobility. Free shipping and a satisfaction-or-money-back guarantee were part of the brand's value proposition.

Wedgwood & Bentley was a growth business, and a profitable one (about a 55% gross margin), with customers in multiple countries. But it never became a big business in this period. There was one factory, albeit frequently expanded with the addition of multiple different "rooms" for different types of product and different parts of the production process, arranged in sequence to provide an efficient production line. It was self-funded from cash flow. Revenue peaked at about the equivalent of $2.5 million in 1810.

British capitalism of the time was typified by similarly structured manufacturing businesses – regionally located with narrow ownership, efficiently employing the automation made possible by new technologies, innovating in production techniques, highly attuned to customer demands and changing trends, differentiated for marketing appeal, and distributed in international markets by importers, wholesalers and dealers, without becoming multinational, mass production giants. They were not yet corporations.

3 Entrepreneurial Ownership: A Golden Age of Corporations

As articulated by Alfred D. Chandler, the great historian of business, a new type of capitalism emerged in the second half of the nineteenth century and early twentieth century, closely associated with a new form of organization: the corporation. This innovation emerged from The Limited Liability Act of 1855 and the Joint Stock Companies Act of 1856 in the United Kingdom. These acts established the fundamental structure of corporations as separate legal entities with limited liability for their stockholders. Although these Acts originated in the United Kingdom, their influence spread quickly to other countries, including the United States, and shaped the development of corporate law and corporate practice worldwide.

We can also think of the new type of capitalism as customer capitalism, since, while legal institutions shaped the structure of corporations, service to the customer and value for the customer were the drivers of their success.

In the nineteenth century, markets were expanding. The United States population grew from 5 million in 1800 to 76 million in 1900. On average, for each of these individuals, in the same period, GDP per capita more than tripled, from $2545 to $8038, making the United States the world's biggest market.

Beyond the statistics, people were engaged in creating a new context and new modes for living: not just a market of unprecedented scale, but new geographical reach, new connectivity via railroads and telegraph, new technologies to utilize, new ways to collaborate and exchange, new shared experiences and new shared realities, a new dynamism and a new mentality about what was possible.

Technology was evolving rapidly, making possible great advances in production – such as continuous integrated production processes for many goods – as well as great advances in consumption – new possibilities in what customers *could* want. The growing, increasingly affluent, technology-aware population constituted demand. Labor, land, and capital were in plentiful supply. The organizational challenge on the supply side lay in the specific combinations of land, labor and capital to meet entirely new demand-side challenges of scale (serving a growing population over an expanding populated geography) and efficiency. The solution to this challenge turned out to be the limited liability corporation.

The Corporation

Although Americans were not the first to form limited liability corporations with widely distributed shareholdings, America was the locus of the first great burst of corporate formation. Between 1783 and 1801, nearly 350 enterprises were incorporated. No such increase occurred in Europe at the time.

The corporate form was essential to aggregate the unprecedented amounts of capital and operating funds required for large-scale railroads, factories, mills, refineries, and pipelines. The managerial revolution that underpinned the administration of these complex organizations was also essential. Corporations were tackling challenges of unprecedented complexity, and management structure and processes were as important to their success as capital. Corporations were an organizational innovation to address the need of customers in the young nation for transportation, banking and insurance, energy, water, food and clothing as they expanded cities and ventured westwards into new territories. Corporations created the transportation infrastructure that citizens needed, as well as required commercial services such as insurance and banking. Corporations competed in the "industries of the future" (Tedlow, 1991, p. 2). They became national enterprises, where none had existed, and many of them became multinational. They became household names and played a significant role in transforming the United States from a society of island communities into a far more homogeneous and integrated community (Wiebe, 1967).

Alfred Chandler (*The Visible Hand: The Managerial Revolution in American Business*) designated the new corporations "integrated industrial organizations," specifically integrating mass production with mass distribution. They combined the economies of high-volume throughput with high inventory turn and generous cash flow. Almost non-existent at the end of the Civil War, these integrated enterprises became the dominant form of value delivery to customers within three decades. In the language of the twenty-first century, they were unicorns.

Market-driven: Applying Technology for the Benefit of Customers

The purpose of the integrated organizations was to serve markets. Chandler considered them a "response to the rise of the mass market" which emerged as a result of transportation and communication infrastructure. The preexisting infrastructure for production, marketing and distribution (family firms and partnerships, wholesalers and resellers, retailers, manufacturers' agents, and various middlemen) was unable to cope with the volume of demand flowing from the newly forming market. The potential of the market impelled producers to adopt mass production machinery; the inadequacies of existing marketers impelled them to integrate forward into marketing, and backward into supply chains. Integrated corporations became the basic infrastructure of the market, and the most important business institution.

Corporations coordinated the flow of agricultural crops from farmers to consumers and finished goods from producers to end-users. They increased the speed of flow of those goods, lowered costs, and improved productivity. In many cases, the corporations added extra customer benefits such as after-sales service, maintenance and repair (e.g., for typewriters and sewing machines), local storage (such as refrigerated warehouses for beef and fresh meat) and financial credit. They innovated to continuously improve the customer experience. The potential of the market drove them. They discovered that branding, advertising and prompt and regular service were market-expanding investments.

An illustration of market focus comes from The National Biscuit Company's 1901 annual report:

> We ... bent our energies ... above all things and before all things, to improving the quality of our goods and the condition in which they should reach the consumer. Knowing that we had something that the consumer wanted, we had to advise the consumer of its existence. We did this by extensive advertising. (Chandler, 1977, p. 334)

The new corporations utilized mass-production continuous flow technology (such as the "automatic line" canning factory operated by H. J. Heinz and Company in Pittsburgh) to bring a greater variety of goods to the national customer base with higher quality, greater reliability, faster speed and lower cost.

Railroads, which made widespread distribution feasible, were themselves exemplars of applying technology for consumer and customer benefit. Construction methods, grading, tunneling, and bridging made direct long-distance transportation possible. Iron rails improved both safety and durability. Ever more sophisticated locomotives increased speed and reliability and passenger coaches increased comfort. For shippers, the railroads provided dependable, scheduled, all-weather transportation with a lower cost per unit of goods moved. One commentator estimated that railroads provided five times as much freight service as canals for an equivalent resource cost (Legerbott, 1966).

The technology of continuous production not only reduced the labor time required for the manufacturing process, it facilitated low unit costs and ushered in the era of widely available appliances such as sewing machines and typewriters. Eventually, of course, it generated the moving assembly line that, in the twentieth century, enabled the manufacturing of affordable automobiles and the era of motor transportation for families and businesses.

Technology was a driver of economic progress. As W. Brian Arthur has pointed out, technology furthers its contribution to the economy through new combinations (Arthur, 2009). These occurred in clusters in the nineteenth century when corporations discovered new applications to benefit the markets they served.

From 1830–1900, roughly one lifetime, GDP per capita in the United States tripled. It's hard for us in the twenty-first century to empathically feel what must have been the happy experience of the accompanying improvement in the quality of life. There were better illumination and better building materials and furnishings and better winter warmth in the average home. Better health, better food and better nutrition, and better clothing. Better schooling. Continuous improvement in communications and transportation so that citizens felt more connected with each other and more engaged in neighborhood, town, city, and civic life. Capitalism touched all American lives through the corporate form and its products, enabling people to improve their lives in many different ways. In a time of consumer belief in a better future, corporations gave reliable reasons to believe and made a lasting and meaningful social impact.

As an example of the application of technology for customer benefit, we can highlight the Quaker Oats brand, a product of American Cereal Company, later to become the Quaker Oats Company. The entrepreneur Henry Crowell was the driver of continuous innovation that served a nationwide and, eventually, international market of both customers (retailers and wholesalers) and consumers. Crowell's customer-benefitting innovations included:

- Steel-cut oats (using a patented machine) in replacement of traditional milling, resulting in an easier-to-prepare product, less contaminated with husks and dust and other residues.
- Soon afterwards, the introduction of rolled oats, with even better preparation characteristics.
- Further innovations such as a puffed rice product, for a wider range of consumer choice.
- The introduction of cardboard packages which were easier to handle, and gave the product greater protection than the bulk barrels in grocery stores that they quickly replaced.

Crowell's stated purpose was the best-quality oatmeal that technology was able to produce. His entrepreneurial instinct was that such a product could compete with local supplies everywhere. His mill was the first in the world to maintain under one roof operations to grade, clean, hull, cut, package and ship oatmeal in a modern assembly line that gave the company a production cost advantage, even with the added expense of cardboard-box packaging. Quaker Oats, according to Crowell, "no matter what the cost, would abandon systems and methods and scrap machinery whenever changes could be made for an improvement of the quality or a lessening of the cost" of the product (Marquette, 1967).

In addition, Crowell pioneered the concept of product branding for foodstuffs, adopting the Quaker symbol (and registering it as a trademark) to communicate purity, neatness, orderliness, wholesomeness and integrity. Quaker Oats brand invested heavily in communications, from preparation instructions and recipes on the package, to extensive print and billboard advertising. Quaker Oats was the first brand to give away free samples door-to-door to generate demand, and also used free premiums, cooking demonstrations and cooking schools, and other forms of publicity. It was also a leader in communicating the benefit of nutrition and health to consumers. Quaker could be said to have pioneered the technique of the brand launch; for example, shipping fifteen carloads of Quaker Oats packages to open the Portland market, preceded by the distribution of free samples in mini-boxes door-to-door prior to the arrival of the commercially packaged product, and accompanied by displays, and shows featuring actors dressed up as "the Quaker man."

Crowell wanted Quaker to be the only brand shoppers requested by name, so that retailers would have confidence to stock it. He understood the concept of consumer sovereignty and developed what today we might call a consumer-centricity ethic in his company that led it to popularity, revenue growth and profitability.

Orchestrating Supply Networks to Raise Customer Expectations

Manufacturers took charge of scheduling the flow of raw and semi-finished supplies from suppliers to their factories when they found that the supply chain services already in place were inadequate to service their high-speed continuous throughput. Then they took charge of scheduling the flow of finished products from the factory to the customer when they found out that wholesalers could not be relied upon to order and inventory products in a way that ensured the customer could always be sure of obtaining what they wanted on time.

The new mass production/mass distribution corporations innovated in organization and structure as well as in business relationships and network building to meet their goal of accurate, timely low-cost delivery and uninterrupted availability for their customers. They approached the development of high-throughput systems via the route of management-as-coordination, specifically the coordination of the flow of goods through production, from raw materials to parts and sub-assemblies to complete products and packaging for well-organized safe and reliable shipping and storage. The goal was not so much economies of scale as high-speed continuous flow through the factory, all the way to the customer.

One solution was organizational. The newly forming multi-functional and multi-divisional administrative structures that entrepreneurial owners were bringing into being included large and well-staffed purchasing departments (including "fieldmen" who bought directly from farmers and producers of raw materials), schedulers, receiving supervisors, factory-flow coordinators, inventory managers, transportation managers, regional distribution supervisors, and communications departments. These complicated inter-connected structures for managing unprecedented complexity were genuine innovations in themselves. They were dynamic and adaptable in the whirlwind of external change in technologies, suppliers, competitive initiatives and, of course, customer wants and preferences as they learned what was possible.

A further evolution of management-as-coordination was vertical integration – if complementary services and suppliers could not be relied upon to maintain the level of high-throughput coordination sought by the entrepreneurial owners, then there was always the option of bringing all the services under one corporate ownership and management umbrella. Corporations like Singer Sewing Machines owned forests and farms, mines, rail links and railcars. Gustavus Swift's meatpacking corporation provides another good example. Swift developed a high-volume "disassembly line" for cattle processing, took ownership in stockyards to ensure input supply, built multiple packing plants to be close to customer markets, designed and built his own refrigerated railcars to transport the beef and maintain its freshness, owned multiple local distribution centers to deepen and widen customer accessibility, and added "peddler routes" using refrigerated vehicles to achieve door-to-door delivery. Growing demand for fresh beef drove Swift to continued expansion of higher and higher speed production facilities and the ancillary supply and distribution chains.

The needs of manufacturers brought into existence a set of supporting business institutions to fine tune the orchestration. One was the credit agency to check the financial reliability and trustworthiness of business partners. Another was the advertising agency, which purchased space for clients in print publications circulating throughout the nation, enabling manufacturers to educate customers in this new age of innovative new products and services and convenient delivery.

Forging Direct Relationships with End-Customers

As the production capacity expanded to keep pace with market demand, corporations scanning the distribution ecosystem of warehousing, wholesalers, distributors, jobbers, re-sellers and retail stores discovered that many of the obstacles to the efficiency of rapid factory throughput were to be found downstream from the factory. Their creative efforts to ensure that the end-user enjoyed all the benefits of low-cost, high-quality production at lower and lower prices resulted in multiple innovations in marketing, communications, and, ultimately, brand-building. The corporations would not have had the terminology to identify their brands, and the trust and reputation that they embodied, as value-generating intellectual property assets, but that is, indeed, what they were creating.

Procter and Gamble (P&G) was an obscure Cincinnati startup in the commodity businesses of candles and soap when it was established in 1837. There were markets for these commodities – the need for illumination and the need for cleanliness – but these markets were unstructured. When P&G was established as a corporation, most American consumers lived and worked on farms in what was more of a barter economy than a money-exchange economy. Certainly, there were no brands. P&G set out, from the beginning, to establish, sustain and grow markets. The corporation was strategically agile in doing so.

P&G, to some extent, originated and most certainly polished the concept of marketing as corporate behavior. First, they cultivated trust with a warranty of full weight and correct tare, appropriately labeled (which was not common) and statements of quality and purity on their products. They supported these statements with research from their R&D activities (which they established at a very early stage) and comparative tests of competitive products in controlled conditions in a company laboratory. James Norris Gamble, son of one of the founders, worked with university research professors to set up the laboratory and conducted research from the consumer's point of view to improve the consumer experience. He experimented with ingredients, formulas, and processes to produce increasingly higher quality products, eventually uncovering a blockbuster: soap so pure it floats.

The floating soap became a brand, Ivory, that required rigidly controlled manufacturing systems to produce consistent and reliable results. The company developed a new, highly integrated and systematic manufacturing and distribution plant called Ivorydale.

When candle sales began to decline in the face of an increasing share of kerosene in the illumination market, P&G shifted strategic focus, resource and investment allocation to Ivory and additional new products and brands, such as soap flakes and soap granules for washing.

P&G expanded geographically through the utilization of the expanding railroad network; the company-owned locomotives, rail cars and feeder lines at Ivorydale optimized the plant as a node on the network.

With national distribution, P&G found that their sales volumes often depended on the behavior and policies of wholesalers and retailers. For example, retailers would not make products available to consumers directly but through requests taken at the general store counter. They could recommend another brand on which they made more profit, even if the consumer asked for Ivory. P&G developed many ways around this roadblock. The first was to package their product in an eye-catching wrapper with the brand name prominently featured along with the performance, purity, and exact weight statements. The second was to reach the consumer directly through magazine advertising (when magazines were becoming the primary communications medium for households). A third was to send free samples directly to homes, along with advertising leaflets extolling the benefits of Ivory and inviting homemakers to be "a patroness for Ivory Soap." The company opened up a new, direct channel of communication that bypassed intervening jobbers and grocers.

P&G was leading the way from commodities to consumer goods, unlearning the habits and assumptions of commodity, batch manufacturing and developing creative ways of taking the lead in the newly emerging national consumer market. The effort gradually coalesced around the concept of brand. Ultimately, product features such as ingredients, quality, and exact weight took second position to the more emotional iconography of purity, femininity, and domesticity. P&G focused strategic energy on the Ivory brand, increasingly investing resources into marketing the brand in order to make it a trusted staple and dedicating measurement and analytical resources to determining the return on the investment. The company cultivated a distinct, recognizable business style, focused on consumers, whom they monitored, studied and assessed, to learn how best to serve an evolving, increasingly affluent, increasingly selective national market. They were creating the "pull" of consumer demand and initiating the consumer society.

At the same time, P&G recognized that developing a community among the company's workforce would benefit business performance. The company gave workers Saturday afternoons off to expand their leisure and family time and, more importantly, formulated a profit-sharing plan to expand the sense of ownership in the enterprise. The first Dividend Day in 1887 saw the distribution of 193 checks. Repeated improvements in the profit-sharing plan were designed for the employees to see the initiative as a substantial declaration of mutual faith and purpose.

Overall, P&G constructed an advantaged knowledge-building and learning proficiency, resulting in a new array of strategic competencies that could be summarized under brand development. Without the tools of scientific market surveys, P&G nevertheless worked resourcefully and continuously to listen and respond to the signals consumers sent. They knew that if they listened better, the resulting knowledge would help their brands win in the marketplace. The company created and launched new brands so that, by the early 1900s, P&G was a portfolio of intensively researched and intensively marketed consumer brands.

Entrepreneurial Ownership

Entrepreneurship is the economic function that drives the capitalist system to higher levels of performance by identifying the unfulfilled desire of customers for better and better user experiences and meeting that need via innovative new products and services. It is the pursuit of new economic value – a pursuit because success is not guaranteed and may not even be the most common outcome of entrepreneurial initiatives. It is, therefore, common to link the economic function of entrepreneurship to the unusual individuals who are willing to bear the uncertainty of outcomes and take the risk of spending time and money on innovative projects.

The entrepreneurs who created the market-leading enterprises of the nineteenth century, along with their families and chosen associates, continued to control them. They personally held nearly all the voting stock in their companies. They turned over the day-to-day operating management to full-time salaried managers, while retaining longer term decision rights over investment, resource allocation, and top management recruitment.

Many of the names of the owner-entrepreneurs survive to this day: Rockefeller, Carnegie, Vanderbilt, Morgan, and more. Some of them are vilified by historians and journalists who disagree with how they made money. They called them Robber Barons – one of the images that still survive as an ill-informed commentary on capitalism.

Let's briefly look at one of them, John D. Rockefeller. According to one historian, "Rockefeller had a fixation for honest business" (Folsom, 2013).

Before 1870, only the rich could afford whale oil and candles. The rest had to go to bed early to save money. Rockefeller's Standard Oil enabled working class people nationwide to afford to light their homes at night. A Standard Oil business communication included this mission statement:

> I may claim for petroleum that it is something of a civilizer, as promoting among the poorest classes of these countries a host of evening occupations, industrial, educational, and recreative, not feasible prior to its introduction, and if it has brought a fair reward to the capital ventured in its development, it has also carried more cheap comfort into more poor homes than almost any discovery of modern times. (Folsom, 2013)

Rockefeller was a first-mover entrepreneur willing to make big investment bets in a fast-growing industry, in order to be the first player to reap the economies of scale that he recognized were the key to the economics of the business. He also realized that high volume and rapid throughput in his refineries – just the same as the high-volume production, high-volume distribution manufacturing companies described by Chandler – were necessary to keep unit costs low. High throughput could be best supported by low prices to the consumer. The effects of low-cost illumination on American productivity and quality of life are incalculable, but undoubtedly the extra hours for working, studying, and family time were part of the formula for economic growth.

His company built the world's largest refinery and cut unit production costs by more than half. It discovered the cost control benefits of backward integration, such as building its own barrel works, saving $1.25 per barrel on a volume of 3.5 million barrels. It discovered product portfolio expansion, finding ways to convert petroleum fractions into salable products such as lubricating oils, paraffin for home canning, naphtha for road surfacing and gasoline.

Rockefeller achieved his mission through an entrepreneurial orientation. He decided to become the biggest and best refiner in the world. He employed R&D researchers and chemists to extract more consumable products from every barrel of crude oil. He pursued industry integration to most fully utilize the ability of the best engineers and managers. He ensured that the familiar blue barrels of Standard Oil's products were of the highest quality. Pumps, buckets, and tools were all clean and under constant inspection; no litter was tolerated in a Standard Oil plant. Nothing was left undone to make the Standard Oil products, per Rockefeller's long-standing policy, attractive to the consumer.

Rockefeller paid higher than market wages because he believed it helped reduce long-run costs. He generated trust among his top managers and made sure they took care of their health, gave them long vacations and paid leave. He valued their ideas. His goal was to assemble the highest-performing teams composed of the best people.

He was one of the entrepreneurs of the second half of the nineteenth century who defined the market entrepreneurship of the time: a clear vision of the customer and the benefits that they would value, a commitment to efficiency in order to deliver low prices, an understanding of the need for process coordination for the uninterrupted high-speed throughput required for that efficiency, and the long term perspective to invest in both production capital and working capital, including R&D, marketing and management.

British historian Paul Johnson calls Rockefeller and his peer entrepreneurs "The Prospering Fathers":

> a "collection of entrepreneurial individualists united only by their colossal energy, native shrewdness and belief in their country's future, transformed a predominantly agricultural society into an industrial and financial super-state, laying the foundations of the nation's geopolitical supremacy and of what has rightly been called the American Century." (Johnson, 2001)

Of Rockefeller's Standard Oil, Johnson wrote that no other "has done so much for the ordinary consumer." He refers not only to the reductions in the cost of kerosene, "the staple of housewives throughout the nation," but also the long run contribution of cheap oil to the generation of electricity, transforming the far west of America into one of the world's most efficient industrial zones, as well as the even greater contribution to the automobile revolution that ended the isolation of scattered farming families and set industrial workers on the road to comfort and affluence.

Capitalizing Cash Flow

The mass production and distribution system resulted in high stock turn and generous cash flow. This cash flow often covered the needs of both working capital and investment capital and left sufficient funds for dividend payments. Chandler tells the story of Diamond Match Company, which developed and installed "modern, continuous, automatic match machine(s) . . . that revolutionized the match industry." The company also developed comparable machines for the manufacture of paperboard and strawboard boxes. By the early 1890s, seventy-five workers could produce 2 million filled matchboxes per day, an output that would have required 500 workers prior to the introduction of the new machines. All of this domestic expansion was financed from retained earnings alone. Even during the depressed years of the 1890s, Diamond Match Company continued to pay a common stock dividend of 10 percent. The prices of matches to the consumer did not rise.

Another contemporary case study for internal financing from cash flow is that of Singer Sewing Machines. Singer built by far the largest sewing machine factory in the world at Elizabethport, New Jersey in 1874 – and subsequently expanded it. Singer built an even bigger factory in Kilbowie, Scotland in 1885. It acquired its own timberlands and some transportation facilities. All of Singer's extensive physical capital investments – its two great factories, a cabinet-making facility and a metal foundry, as well as forests and transportation equipment – were financed out of current earnings. The company often had a cash surplus to invest in government bonds. There was no need to go to the capital markets for long-term credit.

Dynamic Efficiency

In their search for business efficiency, the corporations of the nineteenth century had no precedents or case studies to consult. Many initially pursued efficiency via horizontal combination, buying or merging with other firms in their industry producing the same or similar goods. But this form of horizontal combination rarely proved a viable long-term business strategy. Efficient businesses abandoned this route and adopted a vertical integration strategy, reaching back into the supply network to ensure a smooth flow of inbound commodities and parts and reaching forward into the distribution network to ensure a smooth flow of finished product to customers and consumers. The combination of upstream and downstream control complemented the high-throughput continuous production factories.

To the Chandlerian combination of mass production plus mass distribution, Richard Sears and the Sears Roebuck Company added the novel innovation of mass merchandising, reaching many millions of customers, many of them rural, across the USA, and coordinating their demand on behalf of manufacturers and suppliers. The Sears system developed customers and distribution methods for small manufacturers, smoothing out their demand curves and making them more predictable. Farmers in California wanted ploughs made of Pittsburgh steel and ranchers in Montana wanted baling wire made in Toledo, and home-makers in Oregon wanted sewing machines made in New Jersey. Sears har-nessed their purchasing power and secured supply on their behalf at the low prices the company could command as a result of volume buying.

These end-customers had become dissatisfied with the high prices that resulted from middlemen – such as the local General Store – marking up goods merely for receiving and stocking them, and so they welcomed Sears' mail-order retailing innovation with great enthusiasm. Sears perfected a new dynamically efficient business model – low prices, low margin, low overhead, and heavy advertising to drive high throughput – that benefitted the consumer and the supplier, and played a large role (as did P&G's direct-to-consumer branding) in bringing a consumer society into being.

A significant component of the new business model was the contribution to volume throughput of advertising, both through the mail-order catalogue and the direct-response advertising in magazines. Richard Sears wrote the advertis-ing copy himself, and experimented with the exact wording and phrasing that would draw the greatest response. He discovered the power of low advertised pricing, and always strove to offer his customers the lowest prices, and invited price comparisons. He often guaranteed the lowest prices on selected items. He perfected techniques of targeting (e.g., rural farmers through their group pur-chasing organizations called Granges) and positioning. He originated many merchandising techniques that remain familiar to this day – membership models, frequent purchaser discounts, free premiums, bonus items, and many more. He devised a form of ad tracking, asking customers to indicate the magazine in which they had seen a Sears advertisement. He ran cost-per-order tracking for every catalog and advertising program, so as to be able to compare efficiencies across media and refine his economic calculation.

Richard Sears, as the entrepreneur at the helm of Sears Roebuck, grew the business rapidly by exploring, through experimentation, what value his target customers were seeking, using as many experimental initiatives as he could think of. He started in the mail order business with watches, which he could buy low and sell slightly higher. He gave railroad station agents a sales commission to be part of the distribution system. He soon found that he could buy watch parts and mechanisms and assemble them rather than procure finished watches, and thereby offer lower prices and achieve greater volume. He added jewelry, clothing, sewing machines, cream separators, organs and pianos, sporting goods, bicycles, harness and saddles, furniture, china and glassware, and many more lines (Jeuck, 1950; Advertising Age, 1988; Klein, 1993; Dyer et al., 2004). Insofar as capitalism is a process of continuous, organic change, Sears Roebuck exemplified it.

Every action was taken for a purpose: to learn more about what the target customer, especially the rural farmer, wanted to buy and to supply it at the lowest possible cost and highest speed. Sears Roebuck's implementation of its purpose embraced rapid accumulation of increased specialized knowledge about the distribution and merchandising system, and the building of capacity to sustain the system (larger catalogs, heavier advertising schedules, bigger promotion drives, larger warehouses and more efficient order fulfillment, more resellers). In today's language, Sears Roebuck demonstrated and sustained great agility.

Cost Reduction Resulted in Price Reduction

A significant result of this pursuit of dynamic efficiency through vertical integration was lower prices for end-users. The wholesale price index in the US fell from 151 in 1869 to 82 in 1886. On farm products, the price index fell from 128 to 68 in the same period, and on metal and metal products from 227 to 110.

From 1870–1897, the price of kerosene fell from 26 cents per gallon to about 6 cents – and the kerosene of 1897 was much improved in quality and performance over that of 1870 (McGee, 1958).

The increased supply of goods and services emanating from the integrated corporations had the result of reducing transportation prices. In all of the nineteenth century except for periods of wartime inflation, the general trend of railroad freight prices was downward. In relation to other falling prices, the fall in railroad freight rates was truly remarkable. Over the decades, the nominal railroad rates fell by one-half to two-thirds. The price for shipping wheat from Chicago to New York fell from 65 cents per 100 pounds in 1866 to 20 cents thirty-one years later. Dressed beef shipments between the two cities fell from 90 cents per 100 pounds in 1872 to 40 cents by the end of the century. In westbound traffic from New York to Chicago, the most expensive, or Class 1 goods, fell in price from $2.15 per 100 pounds in the spring of 1865, to $.75 at the end of 1888. Class 4 goods fell, during the same period, from $.96 to $.35. The most remarkable rate cuts occurred during the great rate wars of 1876–77, between the great trunk lines, soon after the completion of the Baltimore & Ohio route to Chicago in 1874. Class 1 rates fell, in those two years, from $.75 to $.25 per 100 pounds, while class 4 rates fell to $.16. Eastbound freight rates from Chicago to New York dropped phenomenally by 85 percent, from $1.00 to $.15. Passenger rates were cut in half in this period. Real freight rates were also lowered by improving the services supplied by the railroads, such as providing storage or carting services without charge (Rothbard, 2017).

NBER's analysis (Fishlow, 1966) estimates that, by 1910, "real freight rates [had fallen by] more than 80 percent from their 1849 level, and real passenger charges 50 percent" (p. 19).

One of the most poorly directed criticisms of the corporations of the nineteenth century is that they used pricing as a weapon to destroy rivals who weren't quite so efficient and could not offer their customers low prices. The relentless pursuit of efficiency and the enthusiastic adoption of rapidly advancing production technologies and organizational streamlining were among the causes of the fall in consumer prices, which the entrepreneurs embraced as a stimulus for increased unit sales and revenue growth. The consumer was a big winner in reduced prices for illumination, packaged food and meats, clothing, homebuilding materials and furnishings, mail, and cleanliness and hygiene. Manufacturing companies and farmers enjoyed a similar trend in price production for wood and metal products, machine parts, office equipment, transportation, nails, screws, axes, hoes, and saws.

The firms that succeeded did so largely because their operational effectiveness and scale efficiencies based on new technology, organizational innovation and refined production processes delivered better quality to customers at lower prices. Accusations of predatory pricing and anti-competitive behavior are inappropriate.

Prevailing Economics

The prevailing theories of economics at the time can be described under the heading of classical economics. As noted above, Adam Smith was the founding father of this school of economics, with Richard Cantillon preceding him in identifying entrepreneurship as the driving force of the market system, a human actor Smith variously referred to as an "undertaker" of projects (translating literally from Cantillon's French) or a "projector."

The micro-economics of entrepreneurs purposefully combining and recombining assets to produce outputs perceived as valuable by customers were set out by Carl Menger in Austria, Philip Wicksteed in England and John Bates Clark in the US. While academicians were by no means as influential in economic thinking as they were to become in the twentieth century, whatever influence they had was in favor of markets and entrepreneurship rather than government intervention, central planning and regulation.

Entrepreneurship was viewed positively as honest labor, doing the hard work of gathering and arranging resources for production, and doing it well. Managerial organization was considered the necessary coordinating function for production. Competition was viewed as an engine of progress and capital as "a tool in the hand of working humanity" (Clark, 1899). The Keynesian revolution in economic theory, characterizing private entrepreneurship and corporations as responsible for instability, was yet to arrive, and theories of principal/agent conflict had not yet surfaced. It was not until the First World War and the revolution in Russia that ownership and management became viewed through a class lens or that management was seen as a tool for organizing production for society as opposed to the corporation.

The "robber baron" critique of entrepreneurial capitalism was a product of journalists rather than economists. Similarly, the antitrust movement that brought the Sherman Act legislation in 1890 was political and did not originate with, nor was it supported by, the economists of the time.

John Bates Clark wrote: "Combinations have their roots in the nature of social industry and are normal in their origin, their development, and their practical working. They are neither to be deprecated by scientists nor suppressed by legislators." Simon N. Patten of the Wharton School also defended the trusts: "The concentration of capital does not cause any economic disadvantages to the community. Those . . . .combinations are much more efficient than were the small producers whom they replaced." And David A. Wells said: "Society . . . has got to abandon . . . the prohibition of industrial concentration and combinations. The world demands abundance of commodities, and demands them cheaply; and experience shows that it can have them only by employment of great capital upon the extensive scale" (Di Lorenzo, 1985).

A contemporary survey by Sanford D. Gordon concluded that a "big majority" of economists at the time held a dynamic view of the competitive process and saw business combination and merger waves as a competitive device aimed at capitalizing on the newly advanced technologies of large-scale production. The results were output expansion and lower prices, precisely the opposite of what future monopoly theorists would claim.

Unentangled with Government

At the turn of the nineteenth century into the twentieth, US Executive Branch civilian employment was 231,000. Today's federal government employment numbers more than 10 times that. Federal outlays were $525 million (in today's dollars); they're projected to be more than 1,000 times that figure in 2022. In 1900, the departments of Labor, Commerce, HHS, HUD, Transportation, Energy, Education, and Veterans' Affairs did not exist. There was no EPA or SBA or National Intelligence Agency. There wasn't much government with which corporations could be entangled.

The Federal Government did involve itself with corporations, of course. The Sherman Antitrust Act of 1890 was the Federal Government's weapon of choice to arbitrate issues of horizontal consolidation and industry concentration. The Interstate Commerce Act of 1887 was to control prices for freight-hauling on railroads. But business legislation at the federal level was quite rare in this period (Openstax, 2022); the administrative state had not penetrated deeply into the commercial activities of the business world, and corporations saw no need to invest in the kind of lobbying for a comfortable position in the state's embrace that we see today.

The railroad industry was an exception to the principle of separation from government. The capital cost of creating railroads was disproportionately large compared to all other undertakings, and this problem was solved with government land grants and government-issued or government-backed bonds. The land grants were corrupt from the beginning since the railroad companies typically kept a part of the land they were granted for right-of-way and re-sold the rest to translate the capital grant into spendable revenue. Added to this form of corrupt entanglement was the complication of the federal government granting land that had been confiscated from American Indian tribes without an agreed contract in place.

This exception to the ethical conduct of corporate business was a danger sign for the future. But for now, it was not the norm.

American Divergence: Shared Roots, Distinct Paths

The entrepreneurial ownership pathway to customer capitalism in the United States diverged from the development of capitalism in emerging economies worldwide.

Japan was clearly capitalist in the sense that its economy was based on private property and a relatively high level of economic freedom. Its modern business sector began to grow in the late 1880s (McCraw, 1997) and a key institution in this growth was the zaibatsu (literally "financial clique") (Addicott, 2017). In these conglomerates, innovation and diversification took place at the group level, and individual firms remained small and undiversified relative to their US counterparts. They did not integrate forward into distribution or backward into the supply chain. They depended on external retail and wholesale firms to distribute and market their products. These features of Japanese corporations have persisted until the present day (Fruin, 1992).

German industry also shows a distinctive development phase in the late nineteenth century. The great coal, iron and steel ventures that grew up around the Ruhr River, including Krupp, Stinnes, and Bochumer Verein, were associated with the growth of so-called universal banks, such as Deutsche Bank (formed 1870) and Dresdner Bank (formed 1872), which concentrated on financing the development of large-scale industry, exerted in the form of "development assistance to the strong" (Tilly, 1986). These banks gradually increased their direct influence over capital-intensive firms relative to the founding entrepreneurs. Bank executives sat on supervisory boards with full participation in strategic decision-making, including approval of future investments. The banks also accumulated proxy voting rights – the right to vote on all shares deposited by other shareholders with that bank.

Co-operative groups such as the Association of German Engineers, the Association of German Iron and Steelmakers and the Association of German Machine Engineering Firms were formed in the late nineteenth century and exerted a collective knowledge-sharing influence in a form of co-operative capitalism (McCraw, 1997). Cartels – ranging from "gentlemen's agreements" to well-organized syndicates – were a feature of this German form of capitalism, aimed at avoiding "ruinous" competition and governing production quotas and pricing (McCraw, 1997, p. 148). Even an IG (*Interressengemeinschaft* or "community of interest"), which resembled an American holding company, was a coalition of firms that gave up entrepreneurial autonomy in return for the group protection of profit-pooling and cost and price controls. Cartels were seen as a form of "co-operative self-help," favorably compared to the ruthless American practice of "throwing workers into the streets" (Liefmann, 1910)

Great Britain was in a different situation to Germany and Japan at the end of the nineteenth century, in the sense that a large percentage of available capital was invested in its colonies and in Latin America. In addition, the country was at a disadvantage in the second industrial revolution compared to its ascendance in the first, in that it had no large companies in those industries most advantaged by what Alfred D. Chandler called the economies of scale and scope. The entrepreneurial innovation exhibited by Josiah Wedgwood and the hordes of entrepreneurs who entered markets around the same time did not develop in the same direction as the large-scale firms in the United States. Consequently, Britain fell far behind America in terms of productive capabilities in major industries.

The American path of entrepreneurial ownership to big business was undeniably distinct. This model of entrepreneurial capitalism, marked by its dynamic and competitive nature, remains a defining feature of the nation's economic history and continues to influence business practices and innovation worldwide.

A Golden Age

We can view the second half of the nineteenth century as the period of growth and maturation of a golden age marked by the ascendancy of corporations and the emergence of customer-centric capitalism. Historian Carlota Perez tracks the multiple successive phases of several technological revolutions in history, encompassing periods of gestation, configuration, innovation, market development, and eventual maturity, spanning around half a century. She terms the maturity "a Golden Age," when all the new products have been introduced, new industries and new systems have emerged, and full potential, while not yet realized, can be contemplated (Perez, 2002).

By the early twentieth century, the United States enjoyed a Golden Age of corporations. An organizational revolution had revamped the basic structure of the economy and society, gestating around the middle of the nineteenth century, configuring quickly in the following decades, innovating in multiple directions, creating and satisfying markets, and beginning to mature.

Maury Klein described the Golden Age as a "society of organizations" (Klein, 1993). Complicated activity systems everywhere in society required planning and co-ordination to operate efficiently, and corporations showed the way and perfected the methods. The success of creative entrepreneurs imagining industrial enterprises of enormous size and subsequently mastering ways of administering them reshaped the structures of economic institutions. The corporation replaced partnerships, and proprietorships and became the general vehicle for private enterprise. There was plenty of trial and error in this transition, and plenty of flaws that demanded correction, but we can nevertheless conclude that the corporations that succeeded exhibited the four-fold purpose that drives value creation and capitalist progress, an ongoing process of application of purposeful principles:

- An inspiring vision: corporations looked forward to a better future for their customers, whether in the home, on the farm, in the city or in the factory, and focused their resources and ingenuity on bringing it about.
- Prosperity through efficiency and innovation: corporations drove relentlessly to lower costs and improve their speed and efficiency of throughput in mass production and mass distribution while at the same time bringing product and service improvements to market at a rapid pace, and they earned customer loyalty by doing so.

- Win-win relationships: corporations understood the many partnerships that enabled their prosperity, from the supply chain to customers, and they provided value for all their partners.
- Taking care of future generations: all Americans, including those who owned and managed corporations, kept an eye on the future that held so much promise for betterment. Carnegie, for example, envisioned virtually limitless uses for iron and steel for rails, bridges, and multistoried buildings that would transform cities and improve lives. Henry Ford envisioned an automobile that anyone could afford, opening the way to unprecedented mobility. These entrepreneurs and countless others created new knowledge that future generations could utilize and enhance.

Customers' lives were transformed from rural isolation in a barter economy to beneficial participation in a great national and international value creation network, in which commodities were converted into easily available value-added products and services from light to nutrition to cleaning to clothing to home appliances.

Whatever their imperfections in this period of emergent corporate growth, the newly emerging organizations revealed for the first time what an enormous positive influence corporations can exert on the material progress, fortunes, and feelings of well-being of an entire country and all its citizens. The nation depended on their ability to harness the potential of the new technological innovations that were being discovered and transform that potential into productivity and wealth. The performance of the corporations *was* the national economic performance.

The corporations and the customer benefits they refined and distributed were emergent properties of capitalism. In the context of private ownership and the freedom of entrepreneurial innovators to retain and reinvest the profits of their innovative initiatives, they gestated and nurtured and made possible the new form of capitalism that Chandler identified, one that we can call customer capitalism in recognition of the primary focus and primary beneficiary.

4 The Early Twentieth Century: One Step Forward, Two Steps Back

In the first part of the twentieth century, the management organizations that had inherited control of corporations from their entrepreneurial founders and leaders made further advances on customer capitalism via multiple innovation streams; they refined organizational structures to better serve customers, adapted organizational processes for multi-national tailoring to local tastes and demands, and created more customer-focused processes.

Germany and the Multi-Divisional Model for Multinational Application

The early twentieth century saw the accelerated internationalization of the production, marketing and distribution of corporate organizations. Chandler picks out German entrepreneurs for their leadership in investing in production facilities and management sufficient to achieve economies of scale and scope via product-specific international marketing and distribution facilities and, equally, via the essential management structures and processes through which the originating entrepreneurs shared control and decision-making. German companies became first-movers in many of the new capital-intensive industries of the second industrial revolution, not only in Germany but in all of Europe and beyond. German firms' organizational capabilities gave them advantages in international markets and enabled quick recovery and further acceleration after the 1914–24 decade of war and post-war crises.

While many German enterprises focused on production goods rather than consumer goods, customer and market focus played a major role in their international ascent. Gebruder Stollwerk, a maker of chocolate ingredients and coatings, grew internationally by paying exceptionally close attention to marketing, including packaging to preserve quality, branding, and advertising. They created a network of branch sales offices throughout Europe and the United States to stay close to customers and transmit information on local tastes and demands. Local factories outside Germany were built to support its local marketing organization rather than the other way round. Stollwerk expanded into adjacent markets, such as vending machines, to help customers automate and expand sales of their products.

The dynamic growth in foreign markets and related industries was enabled by giving managers the title of *Prokurist*, a manager legally empowered to act as a company owner. An extensive central staff oversaw bookkeeping and cost accounting, and shaped operational standardization, while the *Prokurists* were able to take local initiatives and tailor services to local customers.

Similarly, storage battery maker AFA (Accumulatoren-Fabrik AG) was a German manufacturer that built an international corporate organization to leave British and French producers far behind in the developing market for components of power generation and transmission systems. Their leadership came through the establishment of a multinational network of divisions and branch offices to market, install and service batteries under a maintenance contract. AFA's multiple national subsidiaries each had their own close-to-the-customer sales and service organizations, while Berlin HQ administered operations through centralized divisions for inspection, process development, marketing and sales planning. There was a published organization chart (at a time when few British companies had "even an informal sketch of its organization," according to Chandler) accompanied by 100 pages of text defining functions and the relationships between them. International trade counted for German firms like AFA, and a highly tuned multi-divisional, multi-country organization with a strong commitment to marketing and innovation was carefully designed for that purpose. Part of the design was hiring American engineers, researchers and managers to help reproduce the "American system of manufacturing."

Another German firm, Siemens, established the most intricate and extensive industrial complex in the world in Berlin, with a single corporate administrative office managing a worldwide network of marketing, service, customer relations and distribution. With its six sales divisions, multiple autonomous production divisions, and centralized administrative functions, Siemens was, to a significant degree, the forerunner of the multidivisional structure that DuPont and General Motors fashioned in the United States.

GM's Innovative Multi-Divisional Structure

The evolution of the corporation continued in the U.S. with new advances in the early years of the twentieth century. To bring the poorly organized firm of General Motors into the forefront of this evolution, a new management team installed by entrepreneur and GM president Pierre du Pont established an innovative new divisional structure in which each division's purpose and activities were defined according to the customer market it served.

The chief assistant to the GM President, Alfred P. Sloan, is credited with the realization that Americans viewed the purchase and ownership of their cars as status symbols of their progress up the income scale. GM incorporated this understanding of differentiation in individuals' perceived value of its offerings into both product marketing and corporate structure. The subjective preference structure of customers was translated into the divisional structure of General Motors.

Prior to this innovation, the traditional corporate approach to organizational design had been to structure a large firm not according to its products, but according to functions: purchasing of raw materials, manufacturing, and selling. Purchasing was focused on cost management and efficient supply chain flow; manufacturing on volume, speed of throughput and economies of scale; and selling on mass distribution to absorb and channel the manufacturing output. The executives who oversaw these functions were traditionally given responsibility for all of a company's products, no matter how diverse. If products encountered a change in customer preferences or were a poor fit for the evolving needs of a diverse and rapidly changing marketplace, it was difficult for these functional executives to observe and analyze from their vantage points.

GM's decentralized, multi-divisional corporate structure was built around what today we would call brands – differentiated product lines each with a distinct customer base. Price point served as a proxy for perceived brand status, and GM created a consumer price and prestige ladder from Chevrolet at the lowest price point, through Pontiac, Oldsmobile, Buick, and, at the top, Cadillac. GM claimed that it offered a "car for every purse and purpose." Because the cars were more individually distinctive, they shed some of the perceived stigma of mass production. They were not just means of physical transportation, but became symbols of social standing, personal status, achievement, and financial success.

The divisional structure opened up pathways for different styling, different functions and buyer options, different equipment like wheels and tires, different dealerships, different maintenance and repair ecosystems, all of which were designed and developed to serve the different customer needs identified by each brand and each division. Each division pursued its own customer-focused vertical integration for chassis, engines, parts, body panels, and all the manufacturing and assembly steps to arrive at differentiated finished cars.

Each division was headed by a chief executive given a high degree of autonomy by the GM central office, with a P&L responsibility and control over decisions in operations, purchasing, manufacturing, and marketing. In the 1920s this autonomous divisional structure constituted a radical decentralization for the time, and "an intellectual breakthrough of the first order" (McCraw & Childs, 2018). It took some time for GM to work out the puzzle of centralization versus decentralization, and the driving focus was the customer.

These were the early days of statistical tracking of automobile registrations, analysis of sales data, understanding demographic trends, market research surveys and other customer marketing techniques. Since the GM divisions were tasked with harnessing and forecasting demand, and since each one had a defined slice of the market on which to focus, they worked to refine their customer understanding and to translate it into demand management. They tapped in to the new signals emanating from a consumer society.

One of the GM innovations that arose from its understanding of customer markets was the establishment of GM Acceptance Corporation, a division for financing bulk purchases of cars by dealers and purchases by consumers on credit with installment payment plans. With this innovation, GM empowered consumers and entrepreneurs alike.

With the data flowing from the divisions, the general office was well positioned to devise methodologies to coordinate production with both current and forecasted demand. GM developed so-called "divisional indices" for purchases and delivery schedules for materials, capital equipment required, labor to be hired and estimated returns on investment. Prices, costs and rates of return were calibrated based on customer demand schedules computed with the help of statistics on income, the state of the business cycle, seasonality and market share forecasts, all of which were continually adjusted to actual sales reported by dealers. Forecasting techniques were continually sharpened in what today we might call the application of cybernetics or data analytics.

As a result of the integration of the divisional indices, the GM central office was able to develop financial ratios such as inventory turnover, fixed versus variable costs, and profit as a percentage of sales. Similar techniques were adopted for coordinating flows at General Electric, Westinghouse, and Sears Roebuck, and eventually, such methods were adopted by nearly all large modern businesses in the United States (Chandler, 1977). What Alfred Chandler referred to as the Managerial Revolution was largely driven by the new focus on customers and their needs and preferences captured in the structural innovations and statistical methods of the GM organization.

Procter and Gamble's Brand Management Innovation

A further refinement of customer-focused organizational methods was made with the evolution of the brand management structure and associated processes at Procter and Gamble from 1931 onwards.

P&G established the principle that each one of its brands should be organized as a business, with a single executive in charge and a substantial team of people devoted to thinking exclusively about the brand's customers and their needs and the operational, financial, and marketing activities devoted to meet those needs and generate customer loyalty to a branded offering. Each brand management unit was focused on one brand and one brand exclusively and, therefore, on one customer grouping exclusively. The brand manager was "an entrepreneurial position within the company" (Advertising Age, 1988), charged with monitoring markets and customers, developing business plans and achieving results, raising money (recommending funding via corporate resources), deploying advertising and promotion budgets, directing staff groups, out-performing competitive brands, and managing the brand P&L.

P&G established the principle that the development of a deep understanding of customers and their needs, and of the ecosystem in which these needs were expressed and integrated (such as the running of a household), would result in a competitive advantage through products that were perceived as more appropriately fine-tuned for the jobs consumers wanted to get done (like clothes washing, family hygiene, and skin care) and could earn a premium price compared to less aligned products.

Neil McElroy, the P&G executive credited with the original concept of the brand management structure and associated processes, described his guiding formula as "find out what the consumers want and give it to them." Adopting the goal of finding out what consumers want led to the creation, funding, development, and refinement of a core market research department to provide the brand managers with the best possible information about their actual and potential customers, for them to translate into product innovations, package designs, advertising, and promotions.

P&G invested in a staff of hundreds of researchers and systems of data gathering – essentially, asking questions in door-to-door conversations with homemakers about laundry, cooking, dishwashing, and every other activity for which P&G marketed a product or was considering doing so. Eventually, systems were extended so that the homemakers could use P&G products on their own and report the results and experiences – user-generated data. From these data, the P&G research department developed statistical analyses and forecasts to guide the brand managers. The department pioneered new research techniques such as "day after recall" to assess the effectiveness of brand advertising, focus groups for more efficient collection of first-party qualitative data and sampling techniques from mailed questionnaire responses.

One of the implications of the brand management system is a commitment to long term customer relationship development rather than short term sales maximization. What we now call customer loyalty is a long-term concept for developing and sustaining a strong customer market for existing products as well as the development of an extended platform for the introduction of new ones. The system anticipates ever-increasing quality, efficacy, and innovation and assumes equal effort by competitive brands and therefore accepts the market requirement for continuous improvement. It establishes a context for the expression of the entrepreneurial drive for creating new economic value for customers at the center of the corporation.

The brand management system, and its focus on customers in an identified market segment with jobs to be done and needs to be met, spread widely throughout American business. It was quickly adopted by consumer packaged goods companies, and quickly spread to apparel, chemicals, pharmaceuticals, appliances and electronics, financial services such as insurance, and eventually to business-to-business brands like Du Pont's Kevlar and Tyvek, or Mack trucks and Cummins diesel engines. By the end of the century, computer software and hardware wrapped their complex value propositions and messaging in brands and branded ecosystems, and designed R&D and business models to respond to customers' and consumers' demands.

Two Major Shifts in Direction

In stark contrast to these corporate advances in customer centricity, customer understanding, customer service and customer value creation, the last decades of the first half of the twentieth century produced two major developments that dramatically changed capitalism and pushed corporations in a new direction. The regulation economy of the New Deal and the command economy of World War II changed the attitude of both businessmen and consumers toward capitalism. Capitalism was not the same afterwards.

The New Deal

Politicians declared that the economic downturn of what we now call the Great Depression constituted an emergency of the same character and same dimension as war. In fact, a Supreme Court justice called it "an emergency more serious than war." Politicians, therefore, claimed emergency powers to intervene.

In the era of prosperity prior to the Great Depression, most Americans enjoyed the benefits that capitalism delivered, and businesses basked in the sunlight of social approval. But 1929–1933 brought severe economic contraction. Unemployment reached 25 percent of the workforce, production fell by as much as two-thirds in some categories, banks failed in waves, and the net income of many corporations turned negative. Panic was spreading fast by the time of FDR's inauguration in 1933, and his successive administrations would take on the task of changing capitalism through the mobilization of the powers of the executive and the legislators against "the callous and selfish wrongdoing" of business corporations and the "unscrupulous money changers" of the financial sector (Higgs, 1987).

In a barrage of legislation, regulation, and presidential proclamations, the FDR administration battered down the normal barriers separating business corporations from political control. The government sought to change the way business was conducted. For example, the National Industrial Recovery Act (NIRA) of 1933 empowered the President to approve or impose "codes of fair competition" for every industry. The codes of fair competition covered not only wages, hours and working conditions for employees but also new rules for interstate commerce and detailed specifications for public works projects, and a wide range of compliance requirements. Ultimately, there were over 700 codes covering about 90 percent of industrial businesses with minimum prices and standardization of products and services, as well as employment conditions.

Not only was legislation and regulation directed at changing business practices, the language of politicians and their supporters in newspapers and radio stations changed the descriptive language of capitalism.

"Competition" became "economic cannibalism," and "rugged individualists" became "industrial pirates." Conservative industrialists, veteran antitrusters, and classical economists were all lumped together and branded "social Neanderthalers," "Old Dealers," and "corporals of disaster." The time-honored practice of reducing prices to gain a larger market share became "cutthroat and monopolistic price slashing," and those that engaged in this dastardly activity became "chiselers." Conversely, monopolistic collusion, price agreements, proration, and cartelization became "cooperative" or "associational" activities; and devices that were chiefly designed to eliminate competition bore the euphemistic title, "codes of fair competition." A whole set of favorable collectivist symbols emerged to describe what American law and the courts had previously, under other names, regarded as harmful to society (Hawley, 1966).

There was a concerted effort to rouse patriotic feelings against business corporations. The fate of capitalism was being decided. According to economist Frank Knight, "The public has lost faith ... in the moral validity of market values" (Knight, 1982). Attitudes to the free market form of capitalism, including the commitment to freedom of contract and to profit from the creative allocation of private property, suffered a blow from which they have never recovered.

The War Economy

The coming of the Second World War exacerbated the already centralizing tendencies of the New Deal with more central planning and central control in the government-led establishment of a war economy. In the United States, at least half of industrial output went toward fighting the war, and the remaining civilian economy labored under layers of government burdens and restraints. The federal bureaucracy had acquired power and experience during the New Deal, and businessmen were becoming accustomed to subservience to this bureaucracy. The US command economy of World War II dwarfed all previous experiences of government control, and the same was certainly true in all the major countries involved in the conflict.

To spotlight one example of the many control boards in operation during the war, the Reconstruction Finance Corporation (RFC) had the power to make loans to corporations to direct their activities and to purchase the capital stock of any corporation on terms and conditions determined by the RFC. It had the power to create corporations, purchase land, build factories, and engage in manufacturing itself. The federal government became an investor, producer and commercial dealer, operating subsidiaries including the Metals Reserve Company, Defense Supplies Corporation, Petroleum Reserves Corporation, War Insurance Corporation and many more. Via the War Powers Act, government agencies were able to acquire any real and associated personal property "that shall be deemed necessary for . . . war purposes," and to take immediate possession. This was socialism in the strict sense: government ownership and management of the means of production.

The Office of Price Administration (OPA) produced thousands of rationing boards to allocate resources from gasoline and tires to coffee and canned foods. They engulfed businesses in a maze of red tape and intricate regulations. The Price Administrator could set prices to "prevent unreasonable or exorbitant profits." Some contemporary businesspeople complained that government price controls were an attempt to destroy capitalism (Higgs, 1987). An economy in which resources are allocated and prices set by government directives is not capitalism.

Nevertheless, big corporations supplying the military discovered a good thing, even if it was not free enterprise. According to Professor Robert Higgs, "a hundred firms got two-thirds of the war business; just 33 got about half; and General Motors got about 8%" (Higgs, 1987). It was easier for the government to deal with a few contractors, and the big corporations had the technical and managerial expertise and the large physical facilities to respond readily to government demands. Big business adapted themselves to working smoothly under government command, complying with orders and making what they were told to make, even if greater profits could be earned by making something else. The government fixed prices and controlled the flow of raw materials, set wages and dominated capital markets through war industry financing (Corwin, 1947).

The experience changed the attitudes of leading corporate executives and managers, conditioning them to accept a degree of control they had never contemplated before the war. Moreover, alums of the RFC entered big business including finance, manufacturing, distribution and railroads, and came to power in some of the most important commercial businesses and institutions. Many of the individuals who had enjoyed power and prestige as they progressively expanded and tightened the command system during the war subsequently took the reins in the market economy whose independent systems of transactions and exchange they had previously aimed to control (Jones, 1951).

By the end of the war, the American capitalism of the early twentieth century no longer existed. The dynamics of business took a different course. Joseph Schumpeter, in a 1949 speech, outlined four propositions for the eventual failure of entrepreneurial capitalism: the bureaucratization of large corporations, which would diminish both their productive capacity and their standing; the loss of respect for the underlying principles of capitalism, including property rights and free markets; the hostility of the political and intellectual class, who were not involved in business, toward the capitalist system; and the loss of faith by the general public in traditional values and ideals, giving greater priority to social security and economic engineering in the form of regulation and central planning (Schumpeter, 1950a). While recognizing a residual capitalist vitality, he emphasized that "we have traveled far indeed from the principles of laissez-faire capitalism." The growing role of the state in managing the economy for stability and of the corporation in managing business as a routine would vitiate the processes of innovation, risk-taking under uncertainty and competitive rivalry in continuous improvement.

5 Post-War Capitalism: The Age of Control

Historian Jonathan Levy identifies the "dramatic post-1945 hinge" as the most important moment in the history of American capitalism (Levy, 2021). American companies owned three-quarters of all invested capital in the world, and the regulatory and developmental arms of the New Deal state sought economic hegemony through monetary policy framed by the Bretton Woods agreement and international financial institutions like the World Bank and the IMF.

Corporations, at least in the United States, were able to seize back their investment decision-making, but there was heavy pressure toward fixed, illiquid investment in factories and manufacturing plants for the political purpose of full employment. There was a post-war investment boom, but it was influenced by business's sense of political necessity in an atmosphere of adversarial monitoring of business conduct. In contrast to the energetic and creative entrepreneurship of Rockefeller and Sears and the innovative, customer-dominant logic of Sloan and McElroy, the new capitalist mindset was curtailed and constrained. It was an age of control.

The vision of corporate managerialism became focused on depreciating capital value – bolting immobile production goods to the earth and utilizing labor to consume them in an entropic process of production in which waste and pollution were costs that showed up neither on the profit-and-loss accounts nor the balance sheet. Capital was productive but illiquid and inflexible. Corporate management became an educated and trained bureaucracy. Profits were high, and largely reinvested in current business lines.

Under these conditions, the period 1945–1973 was a productive one. Measured in per capita GNP, the annual US growth rate was 3 percent compared to 1.2% from 1890 to World War II. Measured in output per hour worked, the United States achieved twice the level of most other industrialized nations and accounted for 40 percent of the world's gross production of goods and services, from about one-sixteenth of the world's population (McCraw & Childs, 2018).

There was a significant shift in the work ethic brought about by large corporations. The entrepreneurial ethic of Henry Crowell and Richard Sears was replaced by the social ethic of The Organization Man.

Management Systems – The Case of General Electric Company, 1950–1980

Corporate managerialism and organization man can be represented by General Electric Company (GE), especially from the post-WW2 period to the 1980s.

In 1950, GE manufactured roughly 200,000 different products, competing in 23 of the 26 two-digit SIC industry categories in more than 170 plants in the US and several foreign countries; it employed 250,000 people, with income of more than $150 million on revenue of more than $3 billion. CEO Ralph Cordiner led an organizational restructuring into seven independent divisions comprising 110 companies. To oversee this sprawling operation, GE installed a suite of management systems that typified the era of control and, in fact, were most highly regarded, according to a famous 1981 Harvard Business School case study.

First, there was the Office of the President, a group of top executives directing management from GE's New York City headquarters. The Office of the President was aided by a Services Division – researchers, accountants, controllers, treasurers, and PR executives. From these origins came the development of Strategic Planning. This process required an additional corporate administrative staff comprised of finance, strategic planning, technology, legal and governance components, each headed by a senior vice president. This group then reorganized GE's existing line reporting structure of groups, divisions and departments into strategic business units (SBUs) – but then decided to retain the groups, divisions and departments and superimpose the SBU structure on top of the line reporting structure. An SBU manager would report directly to the Office of the President for strategic planning purposes but to a division manager for operating purposes. Of forty-three SBUs, four were groups, twenty-one were divisions, and eighteen were departments.

Strategic business unit managers prepared annual business plans. Headquarters prepared a list of topics for them to follow. These included:

- Identification and formulation of environmental assumptions of strategic importance. (Environmental refers to the business environment rather than to climate / sustainability issues, as it might today.)
- Identification and in-depth analysis of competitors, including assumptions about their probable strategies.
- Analysis of the SBU's own resources.
- Development and evaluation of strategy alternatives.
- Preparation of the SBU strategic plan, including estimates of capital spending for the next 5 years.
- Preparation of the SBU Operating Plan, which detailed the next year of the SBU plan.

This were also instructions on how the plans were to be presented. There was no direct mention of customers or customer value.

The planning effort had to be staffed, which included hiring an SBU strategic planner, and sending general managers and strategic planners to special strategic planning seminars at GE's Management Development Center. Over time, many of the SBUs developed extensive planning staffs, and by 1980, according the HBR case study, there were approximately 200 senior planners in GE.

Strategic planning cascaded through all GE management systems. Manpower evaluation and selection were keyed to strategic plans. Incentive compensation and performance screens were developed based on the business objectives set out in strategic plans. Strategic planning was ingrained, despite the concerns of operating managers. For example, the HBS case study reveals that surveys unearthed complaints about "cosmetics and upward merchandising of strategic plans" and that "corporate-level reviewers do not understand the businesses well-enough to be competent reviewers." Pressures for current earnings were cited as undermining the strategic planning process: the pressure to provide a steady profit growth and a sustained P/E ratio results in short-term demands on operations which disrupt long-term programs. CEO Reg Jones was quoted as conceding that "we could not achieve the necessary in-depth understanding of the 40-odd SBU plans."

Jones's solution was to add another layer: the sector. SBUs for planning and groups, divisions and departments for operations were all retained, and all were supplemented by the sector structure. This did not bring cohesion. Jones remarked on "serious discontinuities" among the SBU plans, unnecessary duplication, and uncoordinated actions. "At the strategic level, we seemed to be moving in all directions with no sense of focus." Therefore, he introduced another planning concept for the annual cycle: corporate planning challenges. Each year the SBU plans were required to address several specific challenges issued from corporate headquarters. Some of these challenges came from a company-wide study of strengths, weaknesses and needs which ran to sixteen volumes.

There was another company-wide integration mechanism for resource planning, staffed by another group of senior corporate staff executives, who assessed financial, human, technology, and production resources to shape the strategic resource planning challenges.

In 1980, in-depth corporate planning staff analysis resulted in the definition of yet another layer of planning focus: arenas. These focus areas cut across sector, group, division and department lines. They were directed at "getting GE's act together" in energy, communications technology, energy applications, materials and resources, transportation and propulsion, and pervasive services (non-product-related services such as financial, distribution, and construction). Just how this cross-organizational business development would function still had to be worked out.

The intent of strategic planning was control, especially of the financial outcomes the company could report to Wall Street, and of the perception of the company as one with reliable performance and future prospects.

Admired Companies

GE's implementation of control capitalism gained the company the status of "most admired" (Fortune magazine) and "most respected" (Financial Times). The control-oriented model was adopted by the big businesses of the era, albeit occasionally executed in different ways.

At IBM, the codification of control was expressed as "The IBM Way" (Cortada, 2019). IBM's "Basic Beliefs," established by its founder, were formalized and codified into the daily operations of the firm, evolving into standard practices. Each aspect of the company had its own set of policies and procedures. A consistent approach was carefully governed across divisions, functions and geographies. Stringent performance standards were established and closely monitored, and corporate finance and planning controlled both budget and engineering strategies. Issues were "kicked upstairs" to the next level of management in a slow, frustrating and increasingly centralized decision-making process. There were budgets and quotas and financial planning scenarios; planning took place annually from July to November for the subsequent year, with revisions occurring in the spring to respond to volatility in marketplace results. Every few years, a task force was convened to study the problem of the rising tide of bureaucracy, but it seemed intractable.

The era of control was, for a while, a period of revenue growth. IBM crossed the $2 billion mark in sales revenues in 1961 and the $10 billion mark in 1973, reaching $29 billion in 1981. However, profits did not keep pace. They peaked at $6.6 billion in 1984 but began to decline in 1985, falling to $3.7 billion in 1989. The cost of control was high.

Ford Motor Company was another icon in the era of control capitalism. Ford elevated the knowledge and mastery of systems to an unprecedented level, using it as a governance tool that was independent of customers, cars, and the assembly lines on which they were made. Numbers were the keys to the system. An executive could comprehend quantitative aspects of the business but remain detached from its intrinsic nature. In his book, *The Reckoning*, David Halberstam described how the President of the Ford Division, Bob McNamara, could enumerate every statistic that he wanted in a car. When asked what kind of a car he wanted – "hot and sexy ... or comfortable ... or for the young ... or for the middle class ... or what does it feel like" – he had no answer.

Within the company, the tool for control and power was accounting, which was no longer a passive function of counting, recording and reporting, but rather an aggressive function for the relentless pursuit of efficiency and profit. Managing an automobile company was a coldly analytical science based on clinical skills deployed by a powerful, confident internal bureaucracy, staffed by ambitious young people from business schools who knew numbers and systems and how to minimize costs. They inevitably transformed both the company and its purpose. The fast track for advancement in the company, higher pay and bigger bonuses lay in financial management, while the slow track was in design, engineering, and factories. The designers' and engineers' visions for new cars were met with a response in rigid numerical formulations that "cut the gut out of their projects" (Halbertsam, 1986).

The tool for control in Toyota, a successful competitor to Ford and other American automobile manufacturers was the Toyota Flow System, more commonly known as the Toyota Production System (TPS). The development of this innovative operational approach began in the post-WWII era, specifically in the early 1950s, and they were a direct reflection of analytic methods refined as a result of the war's immense demands on logistics, strategy, and operations. The need for rapid innovation and optimization drove developments in areas like operations research, logistics and strategy, and statistical quality control as a means to ensure consistent quality in production lines, which became vital in wartime industries. The war had elevated the critical importance of lean operations, rapid decision-making, and adaptability, all of which were principles that Toyota incorporated.

Post-war, these methods were ripe for application in the civilian industrial context. The ideas and practices of TPS were shaped by Toyota's managers over the subsequent decades, with Just-In-Time (JIT) inventory control and other principles like Total Quality Management gaining significant traction and recognition in the 1970s and 1980s. JIT aimed to minimize waste by ensuring that parts and materials were supplied only as they were needed in the production process. This approach reduced storage costs, eliminated excessive inventory, and increased the responsiveness to market demands.

Beyond JIT, the Toyota Flow System incorporated a holistic approach to manufacturing, emphasizing continuous improvement, employee involvement, and deep analytics to drive decision-making. As the system matured, it expanded to include principles like "kaizen" (continuous improvement) and "jidoka" (automation with a human touch), aiming to perfect not only the manufacturing process but also the overall operational workflow.

This relentless focus on efficiency and quality was emblematic of mid-to-late twentieth-century capitalism, which prized these factors over more direct creation of value for customers. In this era, the belief was that by perfecting the process and product, shareholder value would inherently follow. Toyota's successes with this system had a profound influence on global manufacturing strategies and underscored the period's fixation on efficiency as a core pillar of competitive advantage.

Command and Control

The New Deal and the war economy demonstrated what could be achieved with a command-and-control mindset with supporting control structures and processes. While their implementation took place in the fiat environment of government and therefore were not directly reproducible in private corporations, they set a remarkable precedent. The war machine was built in a short period and delivered on its end goal of victory. There were prodigious feats of production, visible to all. Executives at the head of government agencies established a new tradition of unconstrained authority over resource allocation and production decisions. Direct non-negotiable orders were given to business owners, industrialists, and factory managers and fulfilled to the letter. Control systems were built that reduced costs, shortened timelines, and cut through committee-based consensus mechanisms, brooking no resistance. The War Production Board controlled both what companies produced and what they were not allowed to produce, and had the authority to impose contracts, terms, and conditions on manufacturers. In addition, the Office of Price Administration imposed price controls. Business was seen as an obstructionist villain getting in the way of the war production czars, and the government adopted "its right and duty . . . to disregard the last vestiges of property rights in a time of crisis" (Catton, 1969).

The corporate executives who ventured to Washington to design and operate these control mechanisms returned to their respective industries with the nation's approval and the anticipation of replicating their prior successes in the production of consumer goods and intermediate producer goods, much as they had accomplished with warplanes, ships, landing craft, tanks, weapons, artillery shells and other defense materials. They felt they could overcome any obstacle or difficulty by applying executive and organizational power.

Alfred Sloan, once the great decentralizer, in a post-war speech to the American Manufacturing Association, urged his audience to aggregate their power and implement central planning at the corporate level. This call for centralization was further endorsed by the economics profession, notably led by Professor Keynes, who insisted that wartime mobilization proved the effectiveness of central planning and controls in organizing production. Keynesians who had staffed the Office of Price Administration, the Commerce Department, and the Bureau of The Budget redispersed into the industry to propagate the message of control.

The message became incorporated in the management systems of esteemed companies like IBM and General Electric. It was operationalized in organizational structures, strategic planning, budgeting processes, and accounting controls. In effect, it hardened the arteries of business, creating the conditions for potential future challenges.

Entropy in the Management Ranks

While the business press was declaring admiration for the management systems of the era, economists were beginning to understand that managers and managerial systems respond to motivations that economists would call "non-rational." In theory, creating the greatest amount of customer value in order to maximize profits is the rational behavior of firms and their management teams. However, many economists have observed that managers have other utility functions, possibly best summed up by Nobel prize winner Oliver Williamson: "managers conduct the affairs of the firm so as to attend to their own best interests." He points out that when ownership interests in the firm played the dominant role in determining the firm's activities, the customer value maximization hypothesis is confirmed by the self-interest of the owners. But managers (even if they own some stock) operate on a "general purpose function," which Williamson translates as "manipulating the activities of the firm to conform to their own personal objectives."

He identifies four principal components: (1) salaries and compensation; (2) staff (the size and scope of the department to be managed confer social and professional status, hierarchical power, and perceived security); (3) discretionary spending for investments; (4) management slack absorbed as cost. Slack is defined as spending on costs and payments made in excess of what is required to operate the firm efficiently. Slack comes in many forms: for example, dividends, excess salary and wage compensation, and personal services and luxuries for executives. There can be slack on the demand generation side (e.g., overspending on advertising, promotion, sponsorships and PR, "sandbagging" of expense budgets), on the production side (overspending on plant and inventory, or over-hiring, or inefficient M&A), and in organizational resources (e.g., HR and legal bureaucracies unrelated to customer value creation, and balance sheet cash in excess of customer value creation requirements).

Slack is the means by which management pursues ends other than value creation. Williamson sums it up as *expense preference* (Williamson, 1963): certain classes of expenditure and costs are positively perceived by managers. Indeed, Williamson asserted that managers in subsidiary positions (e.g., in the divisional structures of multi-divisional firms) develop "partisan" goals that are different from those of the enterprise or its customers or even its shareholders (Williamson, 1970). Adding unnecessary staff, inflating advertising budgets, over-spending on R&D and even acquisition activities might be conducted in pursuit of personal goals such as promotion or internal power. As corporations increase in size, their centralized operations lose control over these partisan activities as a result of bounded rationality, administrative overload, incomplete information and compromised communications. The long run entrepreneurial goals of the corporation are undermined.

Lewin and Schiff's empirical research demonstrated how organizational slack hardens into a permanent increase in the corporation's cost base via the annual planning and budgeting process (Schiff & Lewin, 1970, 1974). Managers and controllers pad the annual budget plan with slack, which they can then keep in reserve as the year unfolds, giving it up in budget "savings" adjustments if required in under-performing years, or spending it freely in years of target performance or over-performance. In such years, the slack becomes the baseline of the next period budget and gains permanent status as a planned cost. The corporate cost base inexorably rises, and the corporation becomes more inefficient.

Slack is a form of what economists call "rents" – increases to personal wealth that are not associated with creating wealth for others, the subordination of customer objectives to managerial objectives.

These insights into the way firms make decisions and allocate resources represent a different perspective than that of admirers, and the economists like Williamson, Lewin, and Schiff would see their theory become damaging reality in the next era: the age of financialization.

6 The Age of Financialization

In *Technological Revolutions And Financial Capital,* Carlota Perez identifies negative tendencies in economies when "The general behavior is increasingly geared to favoring the multiplication of financial capital, which moves further and further away from its role as a supporter of real wealth creation." Firms are forced to bend their decisions to provide the high short-term gains required by the stock market. She calls this decoupling of financial capital from production capital a financial "frenzy" (Perez, 2002).

The economic circumstances of the late twentieth/early twenty-first century fit Professor Perez's description well: a period when new technologies and new organizing principles are modernizing part of the economy, while industries, countries, regions, and firms that cannot or will not follow the modernization path are entering a vicious spiral of low growth and lack of funds. The rich get richer and the poor get poorer and financial capital enters this polarized stage as an accelerator of the divisive forces. Finance is diverted from wealth creation into disparate fields of speculation ranging from hedge funds to derivatives to futures markets. The stock market becomes a casino. The revolutionary industries are over-funded, and rampant financial asset appreciation sets in. The imagination of the financiers and the focus of talented and ambitious young people shift to making money from money rather than from production. There is increasing tension between an inflated money economy gone wild and a restructuring real economy.

Undermining the Purpose of the Corporation

The expansion of the financial sector and the frenzied decoupling of financial capital from production capital has resulted in what Professor William Lazonick calls the financialization of the corporation (Lazonick, 2010). From the 1980s, Lazonick maintained that the prevailing business model in the United States broke down because of its own "financialization," an elevation of the stock market and other financial market institutions and components to a position of high influence over the allocation of resources that causes a shift away from long-term reinforcement of productive and innovative enterprise and toward short term financial performance goals. The result is an inequitable and unstable economic performance that undermines the innovative capability of the industry.

The corporations that had shown a pattern of investing in organizational learning and strengthening their capacity to innovate since the nineteenth century turned to speculative manipulation of their stock prices on stock exchanges. One of the most widely employed tools for this manipulation was the practice of stock buybacks. Lazonick has documented numerous cases of the largest companies by market capitalization allocating more than 100 percent of their net income to a combination of buybacks and dividends for stockholders, with buybacks being the dominant element of the combination. This allocation diverts resources away from investment in production capital and innovation projects.

Such a diversion of resources represents a fundamental undermining of the purpose of the corporation. The corporate enterprise is no longer dedicated to the creation of customer value through processes of knowledge-building and learning that can be applied to generate innovative and competitively superior new products and services that improve customers' well-being and satisfaction. The purpose that has replaced customer value creation is the maximization of shareholder value (MSV), which started to become the dominant ideology of how companies should be run from the 1980s onwards. It advocates the distribution of the cash flows that the corporation earns by creating customer value to the shareholders of the corporation before investments in future customer value generation. It is a model for the trading of shares rather than productive investment, since it is the sellers of shares who receive the diverted cash flows. The stock market is not a source of investment capital for corporations, rather a trading casino for financial interests.

Moreover, senior management in corporations – those with the authority to make strategic resource allocation decisions – have been co-opted into the casino and have become part of the MSV problem. This co-option occurs via the HR function through the channel of executive compensation. Over the past three decades or so, stock-based compensation, in the form of stock options and also outright stock grants, has become the dominant component of executive compensation, providing incentives for executives to make corporate allocation decisions, including cash for stock buybacks, that boost the stock prices of the company that employs them.

The mechanism of stock-based compensation is essentially self-dealing. A corporation's board of directors can authorize a stock buyback program, and then management (specifically the CEO, presumably in agreement with the CFO and other C-Suite members) can implement buybacks on the open market on a timing of their choice. Under SEC Rule 10b-18, the company does not need to disclose on which days it makes buyback purchases, which makes it a kind of authorized insider trading. The logical explanation for the prevalence of stock buybacks rests in the ample incentives executives have to do them. The abundant distribution of stock options and stock awards reinforces the incentives.

The Financialized Corporation: GE 1980–2001

GE, an exemplar of the command-and-control era, can provide an example of the financialized corporation. The firm transitioned directly from one style to the next, coincident with the change in CEO from Reg Jones to Jack Welch, two executives as different as chalk and cheese, as Forbes magazine once observed.

The financial engine of Jack Welch's GE was General Electric Credit Corporation (GE Credit), which originated as a vehicle to lend consumers money to buy new GE appliances, charge them interest, and let them pay back over time. Ultimately, it became an enormous moneymaking machine, borrowing money very cheaply in the unsecured short-term markets (via a vehicle known as "commercial paper"), lending the money out at high rates, and profiting on the spread. GE Credit created or acquired multiple financial business lines, such as life and casualty insurance firms and businesses offering home loans and second mortgages, and others in equipment leasing, airplane leasing, financing for commercial real estate, LBO lending, and private label credit cards. The key to the model was GE's AAA credit rating which allowed GE Credit to borrow money at a lower cost than almost any other entity, including banks. GE Credit also provided the means for GE to lower its tax payments, by deducting from GE's pre-tax profits the depreciation on the jets it owned and leased to airlines, along with all the other forms of capital equipment in its industrial leasing portfolio.

GE Credit was a giant of finance that owned and leased the nation's largest fleet of tankers, was the largest lessor of industrial equipment, was a venture capital investor, and financed leveraged buyouts with as much debt and as little equity as possible.

Additionally, both the cash flow and the leverage that GE Credit could sustain funded a plethora of acquisitions. There were hundreds of them, from RCA Corporation, which included National Broadcasting Corporation (NBC), to Tungsram, a Hungarian lighting company, Kemper Corporation, a life insurance and services company, Stewart and Stevenson Services, a manufacturer of gas turbines, Marquette Medical Systems, a manufacturer of medical equipment, and Honeywell International, another conglomerate. The acquisition and subsequent divestiture of Kidder Peabody & Company can be seen as representative of the voracious but undisciplined drive of financialization. Soon after the GE purchase of the company, a series of insider trading schemes came to light as financial scandals, badly damaging GE's reputation. A 1994 bond trading scandal related to the booking of false profits: an accounting profit of $275 million had actually been a $75 million loss. This securities fraud exposed the lack of disciplined oversight of the acquired business, and forced GE to take a $210 million charge to its earnings. GE sold Kidder Peabody in 1995, and Welch called the experience "a headache and an embarrassment from the start."

Meanwhile, in GE's non-financial businesses, the CEO was eliminating whole swaths of jobs when the goal of cost reduction for profit maximization required it.

GE was the number one company in the world in terms of market value for five years, starting in 1993. One of the contributing factors was the unusual ability to deliver on its forecasted earnings growth and dividend payments, quarter after quarter. CEO Jack Welch referred to GE's finance department as "bottom line wizards." The practices that generated the consistency for quarterly earnings growth became known as earnings management. One route to earnings management was using GE's insurance companies as "shock absorbers" (Cohan, 2022). The billions in liquid investments, such as government bonds, that they held, and in which there were embedded gains, could be sold on the demand of the CEO and taken into quarterly earnings. For example, a loss on the sale of the failed investment in Kidder Peabody, which would have put a major dent into forecast earnings, was erased by transferring a similar amount from the reserves of an insurance subsidiary to cover the loss and the potential impact on GE earnings.

The process worked in the other direction too. In 2001, GE offset a big gain from a satellite partnership by taking a similar-sized write-down on a series of failed investments, including a loss on Enron bonds after that company filed for bankruptcy. Managed earnings were smooth earnings.

Bill Gross of PIMCO called GE "a conglomerate financed by a money machine ... .using 'near hedge fund leverage' of seven to eight times and paying investors non-hedge fund risk." Jim Grant of Grant's Interest Rate Observer called GE "an industrial company that has morphed into a financial services company" when commenting on its "exploding balance sheet, profitability and inexplicably consistent earnings growth." Robert Olsen, a hedge fund manager, said that GE's earnings were increasingly derived from "financial engineering" not manufacturing. Ravi Suria, a financial analyst, called GE "little more than a huge, unregulated bank," and a "black box" of earnings of questionable quality turbo-charged by high leverage.

Financialization had distorted the purpose of GE.

Private Equity: Extracting Slack

One of the emergent consequences of managers building up corporate slack and fortifying it in their budget processes was the rise of private equity (PE) funds and the leveraged buyout boom. The investment proposition was the profitable release of trapped capital from inefficient corporations so that it could be put to more productive use by new owners. Slack was the catalyst.

Over time, however, the PE model morphed from one of extracting slack to one of extracting value. This shift involved financial engineering techniques aimed at harvesting an acquired firm's assets (whether productive or unproductive). It also involved cost-cutting measures in R&D investments, shedding liabilities, and diverting the resulting gains to investors. An Element in this series (Feldman and Kenny, forthcoming) documents how the targets of PE funds changed from dismantling the slack-riddled conglomerates of the 1960s to the liquidation of poorly performing assets in existing manufacturing firms in the 1970s–90s, and to the aggressive raiding of publicly traded companies in all sectors in order to provide high returns to the alternative investment portfolios of Wall Street firms, banks, university endowments and pension funds.

7 Institutionalized Control

Institutions are the formal and semi-formal rules and conventions regarding the conduct of business. Institutions are also represented in the organizational arrangements that emerge to guide behaviors in accordance with those rules and conventions. Institutions provide a framework for the evolution of corporate purpose and priorities from customer value creation to shareholder and investor value capture.

Financial Institutions

The institutional role of the stock market in the early years of the twentieth century was to enable owner-entrepreneurs and their partners to realize the maturing of their investments by selling to new owners. Corporate shares remained separated from managerial control over the allocation of corporate resources. So-called "managerial capitalism" was the implementation of this control that saw sustained industrial expansion driven by productive, innovative companies. The management revolution initiated by the entrepreneurial owners of the nineteenth century was continued by professional nonowner corporate management teams in the twentieth century. Management judgment and the enhanced capacity to learn and innovate were combined to generate productivity, and the coordination of complicated processes and structures produced high levels of quality at scale and low cost. The transformation of the institutional role of stock markets to emphasize cash distributions to share traders and top management through buybacks and dividends contradicts the original concept of managerial capitalism.

The concepts of venture capital and the accelerated dash to exit initial investments through an IPO represent a further institutional distortion of the ideas of managerial capitalism. The ever-present concern in the short life cycle of venture capital funded young companies is valuation: the stock price that can be commanded at the IPO and the short time thereafter that is most convenient for stock options and grants to be monetized. While these VC-funded firms don't necessarily represent a large percentage of total financial capital, they are disproportionately influential in the business culture. Venture businesses are a sprint to high valuation in the short term, and the venture heroes are those that fuel and shape that sprint. Strategic management of resource allocations and innovative investments in production capital for the long term are less prestigious.

Another new complexity is the concentration of stock ownership in the cartelized wealth management and pension fund management institutions like Blackrock and Vanguard, and inside the banking industry at corporations such as J.P. Morgan. Through exertion of their voting powers – much greater than those of individual shareholders – their use of influence tools such as ratings and analytical reports, and direct communications with management, the cartel members can influence corporate policy and impact corporate governance. Their priorities are often different than customer value creation, and can include the direct or indirect imposition of restrictions on the granting of investment capital to corporations.

Similar institutionalization of financial capital is exhibited in the form of firms like Berkshire Hathaway, where the corporate purpose is the accumulation of appreciating stock and dividend flows, and where the CEO, Warren Buffet, is feted as a champion of capitalism – a far cry from the Prospering Fathers celebrated by Paul Johnson.

Management Institutions

Business schools and business publishing, the institutions for propagating, standardizing and communicating business philosophy, business practices and business methods, have enthusiastically embraced the primacy of the financial sector, the financialization of corporate purpose and the shareholder value maximization thesis.

The top business schools turn out senior executives for both financial and non-financial corporations, and they advance the techniques and processes of control and prediction. They advocate smoothness – of revenue and earnings growth, of the advance of innovation, and of the transitions in organization and executive succession – and a world where CEO's are rewarded for continuity, steadiness, and regularity, and are wary of the jagged curves of experimental innovation. One element of standard management thinking is the goal of control. It is primarily control of numbers. The compensation of corporate executives is tied to financial performance (as opposed to, for example, the accumulation of value-driving real assets) and they have an incentive to paint a rosy picture of meeting the financial sector's established expectations. And, as Investopedia.com explains, the Financial Accounting Standards Board (FASB) that sets the accounting rules for corporations in the United States provides for a significant amount of interpretation, flexibility, and latitude in accounting provisions. CFOs have a varied accounting palette for painting the financial picture of their company. The Big Four accounting firms who audit financial statements are compensated by the very companies they audit, a direct conflict of interest. Arthur Andersen, the accounting firm for Enron, a firm that entered into a $63 billion bankruptcy in 2001, was a poster child of conflictedness. Andersen and Enron were able to control reporting and remain in accordance with GAAP even though transactions were recorded incorrectly.

The correlate of corporate control for the financial markets is prediction. Securities pricing on markets always includes a discounting of projected future flows of cash or profits. A firm that can convincingly predict future flows will arm the financial analysts, especially on the buy side, with spreadsheet entries for modeling that exude stability and reliability and can be communicated with a high degree of confidence. Ideally, a track record of prediction is built up over time to reinforce the confidence. Corporate executives, within some more traditional firms, who exercise control over resource allocation may decline to fund high-cost innovation projects with uncertain outcomes because they prefer smooth long-term predictions.

The institutions that nurture the combination of control-and-predict management favor status quo maintenance and small increments over innovation-driven major change. Their theory is that economic growth will come from controlled flows projected into the future rather than from the creative and uncertain pursuit of new customer value.

Bureaucracy

A consequence of the tendency toward greater and greater management control in the modern corporation is the growth of bureaucracy, representing one of the most significant transformations associated with capitalism. A corporation with a controlling technocratic bureaucracy is a bird in a cage. In his book *Bureaucracy* (Von Mises, 1944), economist Ludwig von Mises indicated that corporations have an alternative: the market mechanism, in which the consumer is the boss sending value signals to business managers determining what's to be profitably produced, or bureaucratic management in which a set of operating rules provides the guidance. The creativity, empathy and responsiveness of customer capitalism, instead of being coordinated by management as was the case in the Golden Age of the corporation, become constrained by rules-based bureaucratic management.

In a 2017 survey reported in *Harvard Business Review* (Hamel & Zanini, 2017), respondents attributed seven categories of business "drag" to bureaucracy: bloat, friction, insularity, disempowerment, risk aversion, inertia and politicking. The bureaucratic corporation of the twenty-first century is severely hampered compared to the Golden Age corporation of the nineteenth century and diverted and distracted from its focus on customers by internal rules and restrictions. The survey respondents reported that bureaucracy was growing, not shrinking.

The diversions from customer value creation attributable to bureaucracy include:

Diversion of time: Bureaucracy, according to HBR, is a time trap. More than a day a week is taken up by "bureaucratic chores" of complying with internal requests, form filling and interacting with staff functions. Respondents felt that their ability to deliver customer value would be enhanced by a reduction in the number of head office staffers and the tasks they dole out.

Barriers to customer responsiveness: Bureaucracy is the enemy of speed, both in decision-making and responsive action. For example, in large organizations, the time for getting approval for an un-budgeted expenditure was 20 days. Budgeting and budget control are major functions of corporate bureaucracy and a significant barrier to the fast response that is appropriate when customers demand it.

Disempowerment of close-to-the-customer employees: Bureaucratic controls leave few employees with the autonomy to set their own priorities or decide on the best work methods. This is especially applicable to front-line employees who are closest to the customer and know what needs changing if customer needs are not met and customer preferences are not acknowledged.

Disallowing innovation: Bureaucracy greets new ideas with resistance and does not support experimentation. Ultimately, 96 percent of respondents in the survey said it was "not easy" or "very difficult" for a front-line employee to launch a new initiative.

Breeding inertia: In a bureaucracy, programs are implemented top-down. Issues at the customer level are often not big enough to capture top management's attention. Advances toward change fall behind, and it is hard to catch up and break new ground.

Hoarding power and control: Top executives do not want to share power and believe bureaucracy is essential for the control they seek.

The costs of bureaucracy are unmeasured opportunity costs. They lie in unexplored new initiatives, unconsidered organizational redesigns, unlaunched new products and underdeveloped customer relationships.

Why does bureaucracy expand and exert ever-greater control in capitalism's corporations? There are two major reasons.

1. The relentlessly entropic evolution of rules-based systems within corporations. Human systems have always included the insight that devising and applying rules can reduce errors and unexpected occurrences. When management organizations emerged in the railroad industry in the nineteenth century, rules were used to determine, for example, which trains had the right of way on single-line roads. Human discretion took second place, especially when communication was slow between separate locations.

   As the management discipline evolved, practitioners saw more opportunities to develop and apply rules to control far-flung multi-location operations in large scale international corporations. Rules demonstrated the potential to eliminate human error.

   Over time, rules-making became a primary component of the management discipline. Gradually, an increasing number of processes and procedures were transformed into rules-based systems. One of the greatest accelerants of the process was the advent and expansion of the HR department, a channel for rules to be applied to human behaviors.
2. The emergence and evolution of software technology to automate the application of rules. Business Process Automation became a field of administrative management and has recently been supplemented with Robotic Process Management. There has been a growing shift toward requiring humans to conform their actions to rules embedded in software. Software engineers graduating from computer science departments and inhabiting IT departments were not necessarily the right implementers for business systems that affect customer experiences.

David Graeber, a Professor of Anthropology at the London School of Economics, points out that a major negative impact of bureaucracy on the capitalist system is the diversion of potentially productive cognitive and physical labor into unproductive, un-innovative and non-contributing jobs (Graeber, 2019). Graeber defines them as jobs with no point and that make no discernible difference in the world. "Contemporary capitalism," he writes, "seems riddled with such jobs." One estimate cited in his book is that 37–40 percent of all jobs fall into this category. Notably, he identifies many such jobs in the financial sector, where, according to one of his case studies, "in my conservative estimation, eighty percent of (the bank's) sixty thousand staff were not needed." Graeber attributes causality to the form of capitalism in which production is largely carried out within large bureaucratically organized firms in which the upper echelons of bureaucracies in the productive and financial sectors are effectively fused in the pursuit of new ways to monitor, manage, and surveil those actually performing useful work.

Political Institutions

There is an increasing encroachment of political institutions on the business conduct of corporations, often in the guise of mitigating perceived problems of corporate capitalism.

- Environmental, Social, and Governance (ESG) Regulations: These regulations, promoted by various governments, international organizations, and nongovernmental organizations, claim to aim at encouraging sustainable business practices. However, they impose standards and requirements that limit flexibility and potentially affect growth and profit.
- Diversity, Equity, and Inclusion (DEI) Initiatives: These are both governmental and non-governmental efforts designed to limit hiring and employment practices. They represent additional layers of regulation and potential sources of litigation, which can constrain operational flexibility.
- Antitrust Laws: These laws are supposedly designed to prevent monopolies and promote competition, but they are actually a restriction on free-market capitalism.
- Taxation Agencies and Policies: High corporate tax rates and stringent tax policies can be aimed to influence business activities and business choices.
- Financial Regulation Bodies: Organizations like the SEC in the United States, or the FCA in the United Kingdom, impose regulations that they claim will ensure financial stability and transparency. But, as we saw with SEC Rule 10b-18, they often lead to detrimental consequences.

The tolerance of, and indeed embrace of, such institutionalized controls exerted by the political branches, whether governmental, NGO or from other sources, are testament to – and reinforcing of – the declining public confidence in capitalism.

Management

The business discipline – business as taught in business schools and at universities, propounded by consultancies, and written about in business books and periodicals – has inherited the same errors of positivism as economics. All variables are viewed as measurable and suitable for mathematical analysis. The subjectivism of customers' personal preferences and choice-making is dismissed because management as taught in many of today's business schools and practiced by their graduates holds that all variables can be mathematicised and modeled. People can be motivated and manipulated. There is a deterministic agenda and the goal is to control and predict. Entrepreneurial judgment gives way to resource allocation models. Creativity is avoided since it is unreliable and unmanageable while strategy is often expressed in the military terminology of conflicts, battles, taking ground, and winning. "Where to play, and how to win" is a typical description of business strategy, based on bounded industries and fixed total outcomes that must be divided up.

Such thinking about business strategy is not opening up new pathways, perhaps because of a marriage of convenience between executives, business schools, and consultants. Professor Phil Rozenzweig observed that "Managers are busy people, under enormous pressure to deliver higher revenues, greater profits, and ever larger returns for shareholders. They naturally search for ready-made answers, for tidy plug-and-play solutions that might give them a leg up on their rivals. And the people who write business books – consultants and business school professors and strategy gurus – are happy to oblige" (Rosenzweig, 2017).

When Alfred Chandler wrote about entrepreneurial owners innovating in management techniques and structures in order to harness the commercial applications of the new technologies of the nineteenth and early twentieth centuries, he depicted management science leading and directing technological applications. The organization of mass production, mass distribution, and mass marketing was developed to shape the delivery of new value and new experiences to improve the lives of customers. The technologies themselves were of no direct benefit to customers. Management innovation was required to put them to use on the customers' behalf.

Over time and through evolution, technology has increasingly empowered customers more directly. As consumers, they have computing power in their hands and worldwide internet connectivity that enables them to search, discover, evaluate, and purchase. As business customers, they have access to value networks and virtual supply chains and direct global connections that provide the power to assemble and reassemble business assets and business relationships with speed, fluidity, and agility. The control mechanisms and best practices promulgated by management science are less applicable and consensus methods are harder to formulate in this environment because corporations need to adopt a perpetual learning mode and an adaptive approach to responding to their outside-in feedback loops. Bottom-up is not a management mode that can be codified because it is more experiential than orchestrated.

The entire concept of business strategy as taught in many business schools and propounded by some consultancies and authors is flawed by its outcome bias. The mechanism of strategy design is to identify desirable outcomes and then attribute it to a cause: a better strategy, inspired leadership, a winning culture, superior technology, a competitive advantage, a more disciplined execution, and so on.

But the attribution of business outcomes to a designed and fixed strategy is inherently flawed. It is impossible to attribute outcomes to causal factors. They may be the result of choices that were made in the past – for example, to enter this market or that one, to launch this product or that one – by corporations and their competitors, but it is difficult to determine which choices are appropriate under conditions of absolute uncertainty. Feedback is ambiguous. Circumstances are changing.

Attribution of credit for success or failure (an issue that Robert Axelrod and Michael D. Cohen addressed in *Harnessing Complexity* (Cohen & Axelrod, 2000)) is at minimum difficult and prone to error, and may be impossible. The appropriate action proposed by complexity theorists is to "explore and exploit," i.e., run lots of experiments without presupposing which ones, if any, will work, and, if one of them is associated with a successful outcome, invest more resources in exploiting it, until it stops working. Explore and exploit is context-specific to individual firms, and not a strategy that can be codified and standardized for business school teaching. It has become time for managerial science to cede the floor to complexity theory, and to recognize that discovery, not strategy, is the source of business success.

On the other side of the equation, when some practices become associated with past success, they become locked in. As Wardley (2020) explains it, "Over time, companies tend to build up a body of work and processes – the corporate corpus – designed to stop past failure. It's all done with reasonable intentions. The desire to spend money effectively and the desire to know resources are being well used. That mass of good intentions is often the cause of many problems when you try to change the system. That corpus can become a corpse; a zombie killing off innovation whenever it is found."

Wardley defines the problem as "inertia: i.e., we become used to the 'old' and trusted best practice (which is based upon one set of characteristics), and the 'new' practice (based upon a more evolved underlying activity) is less certain, requires learning and investment. Hence, we often have inertia to the underlying change due to governance."

Advances in systems thinking render the cause-and-effect models of traditional management science ephemeral. First, because no single cause or combination of causes can be identified as particularly influential on an outcome; there is too much interaction between agents and processes and customers and competitors to isolate a cause or a bundle of causal factors. Second, systems thinking has identified the phenomenon of emergence: outcomes occur without any clearly traceable relationship to preceding events and conditions.

Capitalism has experienced success with previous business models and management models, from the entrepreneurial ownership model of the golden age of the corporation in the nineteenth century to the scientific managerial models for expanding mass production, mass distribution and mass marketing of the early twentieth century, to the managerial capitalism of the latter part of the twentieth century (see Figure 2). The problem in the current period of aberrant capitalism is that the old models are no longer relevant, and management science and business evolution may not ever be able to generate a new model that's broadly applicable. The evidence from companies like Amazon and Tesla may indicate that firm-specific experimentation and exploration – rather than generally applicable models – are required to open up paths to success.

The applicable model in the era of financialization, the maximization of shareholder value, is a subtractive management model. It does not concern how businesses serve customers, how they innovate, or how they strategize, finance, and organize to learn and bring new knowledge and new real assets to

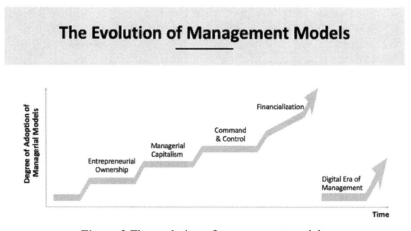

Figure 2 The evolution of management models.

bear on customers' behalf. It does not concern what Professor David Teece (Teece, 2016) has christened the "dynamic capabilities" of building, integrating and reconfiguring internal and external competencies to address changing conditions and create new customer value. MSV is merely a theory of who should receive the residual profits from revenues generated in the marketplace. As Professor Lazonick has pointed out, under MSV the firm may distribute more profit than it actually earns, in the sense of dividend and stock buyback expenditures in a given accounting period adding up to a sum that is greater than the firm's net income.

Entanglement with Government

The definition of capitalism we utilize for this Element includes the private ownership of the means of production, and that assumption continues to hold true for the most part in the United States and the Western economies (although more claims are asserted about the merits of state-led capitalism in China). One of the important threats to capitalism in the West is that the State increasingly constrains the free exercise of private ownership.

One implementation of those constraints is the Federal Register, the published repository of all federal rules and regulations. The Register includes over 80,000 pages, and the cumulative number of final rules published through 2020 is over 300,000 (Crews, 2021). The number of regulations has grown eightfold over the past 50+ years. Economist Thomas Philippon attributes declines in innovation by all businesses, in growth for smaller businesses, and in market entry for new businesses to increases in the scope, scale and stringency of the regulations (Philippon, 2019). The result is increasing industry concentration and declining competition, resulting in lower investment, productivity, and growth.

In this environment of high and increasing regulation, corporations can be seen diverting resources from the end-user as customer and redirecting them toward the government as customer. This shift is evidenced by an increased allocation of resources to lobbying efforts. "Careful investment in a Washington lobbyist can yield enormous returns in the form of taxes avoided or regulations curbed . . . the basis of the economics of lobbying" (Birnbaum, 1993). Lobbying expenditures at the federal level in the United States are several times larger than campaign contributions by political action committees, which are often viewed as an indicator of corporate involvement in the political process, and the distribution of lobbying expenditures is highly skewed to the largest corporations. As Thomas Philippon concludes, "lobbying efforts work," and the largest companies are devoting more and more resources to them.

Another form of entanglement with government is the "revolving door" of executives between government agencies and high-level executive positions in corporations. Researcher Hunter Lewis documented a case of one individual moving from the FDA to Monsanto, then to the USDA, then back to Monsanto, then again to the FDA. While at the FDA, he helped secure approval for Monsanto's genetically engineered bovine growth hormone, including food labeling declaring its safety in milk, and he also allowed GMO foods to enter the food supply unregulated, in opposition to internal FDA findings and recommendations, and findings of independent research, and in contrast to Europe, where GMO products were banned because of consumer safety concerns. This is one of several similar stories from Lewis's research, potentially affecting the health of hundreds of millions of people. End-user customers are not given the highest priority in these cases.

Professor William Lazonick has reported how the adoption by the SEC of Rule 10b-18 to legitimize stock buybacks, which he identifies as a form of "predatory value" extraction that diverted corporate resource allocation decisions from investment in product innovation toward rewards for senior management and other stock traders, occurred after the installation of a Wall Street banker as chair of the SEC. The adoption of Rule 10b-18 was called a "regulatory about-face" from previous SEC views on preventing stock price manipulation.

Ultimately, entanglement dislodges and impedes the workings of value creation for customers within a context of free and competitive markets and replaces them with political markets. Companies focus less on creating the best products and services for customers at the best prices and, instead, pursue economic success through the capacity to harness government power to tilt the game in their favor. To cite just two examples, in 2019, we witnessed a legal battle between Microsoft and Amazon over a $10 billion US Department Of Defense cloud computing contract, and in 2023 we learned about Twitter and Facebook seeking approvals from government departments for their content publishing choices rather than competing in the marketplace for repute.

The outward form of market capitalism is preserved, but its protocols and institutions are subverted by companies seeking preferential treatment from regulators, legislators and governments, whether through tariffs, subsidies, access to "no-bid" contracts, or government-provided credit at below-market interest rates. Lobbying politicians for favors can seem easier than trying to out-compete rivals through innovation and increased efficiency (Gregg, 2022).

Business Schools

Milton Friedman's 1970 essay, "The Social Responsibility of Business Is to Increase Its Profits," in the *New York Times* became one of the most influential works in the field of corporate governance. His assertion that the sole responsibility of a business is to increase profits for its shareholders left an indelible mark on both management theory and practice. Shareholder value maximization became an ideology in business schools.

Friedman's essay arrived at a pivotal moment in corporate history. The 1970s witnessed a shift in the broader economic and political environment with mounting pressures from stagflation, global competition and perceived bureaucratic inefficiencies. Friedman's stance provided a simple, clear, and compelling answer: businesses should focus solely on profit maximization, eliminating distractions from broader societal responsibilities.

- *Academic Influence*: The simplicity and clarity of Friedman's argument resonated within the academic community, particularly in business schools. It offered a quantifiable objective – profit – that could be measured, analyzed, and pursued. In an era where quantitative and empirical approaches were gaining ground in management studies, Friedman's profit-centric view fit neatly. Business schools, aiming to blend rigorous analysis with practical relevance, found in Friedman's doctrine an ideal blend of both.
- *Alignment with Financial Markets*: The 1980s and 1990s were the time of the rise of financialization in the global economy. As capital markets became more influential, the priorities of Wall Street began to dictate corporate strategies. Friedman's shareholder primacy doctrine aligned perfectly with this environment, further reinforcing its appeal. It provided a theoretical backing to the Wall Street mantra of shareholder value.
- *Reinforcement through Compensation*: As William Lazonick pointed out, share buybacks became a popular tool to boost stock prices. In tandem, executive compensations were increasingly tied to stock performance. This created a feedback loop: Friedman's doctrine justified stock price maximization, stock-based compensation incentivized executives to pursue this, and the resulting practices (like buybacks) further entrenched the ideology.
- *Curricular Shifts*: Over time, the curricula of business schools began to reflect this shareholder-centric worldview. Courses in finance, strategy, and corporate governance were increasingly taught from the perspective of maximizing shareholder value. Alternative views, such as stakeholder theory or corporate social responsibility, were often sidelined or presented as secondary considerations.

In essence, Milton Friedman's essay did not just provide an argument – it offered a clear, actionable principle around which businesses could rally. Its alignment with broader economic trends, and its adoption by influential business schools, ensured its position as a quasi-ideological commitment in the world of corporate management. Business schools locked in to this model and persisted with it to the present day (Denning, 2023).

Prevailing Economics

John Maynard Keynes wrote "Practical men who believe themselves to be quite exempt from any intellectual influence, are usually the slaves of some defunct economist." Today, he is the defunct economist to whom many in business are in thrall. That is because Keynesian economics is the default economics that prevails in Western economies.

Entrepreneurship is not recognized as a system driver in Keynesian economics. The emphasis is on centralized planning by governments and bureaucratic and regulatory control of variables to dampen economic fluctuations. The stabilization mentality encourages cost controls and diversification strategies, as well as process management and risk mitigation. Corporate collaboration with the public sector is a favored strategy, both in bidding for government contracts, participating in public–private partnerships and lobbying for sheltering legislation.

The new emphasis on corporate social responsibility in areas such as ESG-guided corporate choices and in business models adapted for climate change concerns reflects, to some extent, the prevalent economic spirit of a major role for public sector influence on private sector resource allocation.

Underpinning the economic interventionism practices of governments are the academic economists' mathematical models, which claim to be able to predict the economic effects of policy interventions. The mathematicization of modern economics represents a loss of empathy with human beings and their purposes and preferences, bypassing creativity and imagination and the value of knowledge and language. Economics has vacated its role as a guide for businesses engaged in customer capitalism.

Distorted Purpose

The American Founding Fathers designed what Professor Samuel Gregg calls a commercial republic, weaving their case for economic liberty into a vision for a free and commercially oriented sovereign nation, exhibiting the moral habits associated with commercial society: freedom, industry, enterprise, competition, entrepreneurship, and trade. Commerce at the time was conducted primarily by individual entrepreneurs, families, and partnerships. They were farmers, crafts-people, traders, and merchants. They set about building the commercial nation; while that was probably never the intent of any one of them individually, it was perceived as a shared purpose.

When corporations took the stage in the nineteenth century, they trans-formed the commercial environment with mass production, mass distribu-tion, and mass marketing. They were intent on building big companies to produce better products and continually lower prices to supply the growing market. Their entrepreneurial proprietors understood that success is "based solely on the wants of the people," as Andrew Carnegie wrote in his "Gospel of Wealth" about the meatpacking company of Gustavus Swift and writing of Montana miner William A. Clark, that he "did not create his wealth, he only dug it out of the mine as the demands of the people gave value to the previously worthless stones." The proprietors also realized that their brand of customer capitalism was good for the nation, a "joint product of the community" (Carnegie, 1906). They were serving customers while con-structing the nation's industrial capacity: more coal being mined, more iron being produced, more sewing machines manufactured, and more mes-sages, goods and people moving from East to West. Their purposes focused on their large-scale corporations, but they were also conscious of building something even bigger. They had ambitions for the nation as well as for themselves.

In the environment cultivated by financialization, politicization, bureaucracy and management control, the purpose of the corporation becomes distorted. The maximization of shareholder value diverts purpose away from capacity building and system building to short term financial goals. Stock prices are quoted every second, transactions are reported daily, revenues monthly, and earnings are announced and reacted to every quarter, bonuses and stock awards are given every year. Employees are hired and let go in rapid cycles of boom and bust, without the understanding of building a loyal, well-trained, highly experienced workforce for competitive advantage. Time horizons are shortened and the next generation is unconsidered.

Short time horizons are the antithesis of purpose. Corporate purpose can be defined on two dimensions: an ambitious, longer-term goal for the company and its customers, employees and partners, linked to an idealistic cast of creating value across multiple generations, i.e. building something bigger than just the firm (Gulati, 2022). The short-termism of stock price management clashes directly with all longer-term ethics, and the purpose of the financialized share-holder value maximizing firm fails the tests of purpose, longer term goals and idealistic multi-generational value.

8 Reimagination

Faced with the realities of financialization, bureaucratization, the failures of management theorizing, the destructive entanglement of corporations with government, the uselessness of prevailing economics, and the distorted purpose of the corporation, how can capitalism move forward? It requires the imagination of a different future.

Restoration of the Primacy of the Customer

The ultimate source of energy in the capitalist system of value creation and betterment is the customer. It is the customer's never-flagging search for improvement in their well-being – in convenience, effectiveness in problem solving, efficiency, greater aesthetic appeal, material and sensual pleasure, health and fitness, personal appearance, social status, career achievement, wealth, productivity, a safer and cleaner environment, and, generally, in their experience of satisfaction – that drives production and innovation.

Consequently, the business model for a corporation operating within the system of market capitalism where customer satisfaction is primary is guided toward three distinctive characteristics:

1. **Creating value for customers**: Value is the economic term for the satisfaction that customers anticipate and subsequently experience when consuming goods and services for which they have paid. The purpose of all businesses is to generate more and more value for customers – to serve them, satisfy them, delight them and meet their needs. By buying and not buying, subscribing and discontinuing, signing and renewing contracts and issuing purchase orders, entering into relationships, customers determine the revenue and profit performance of corporations and customer satisfaction is good business.

   Profit is an outcome of serving customers effectively and efficiently. It's a signal from customers that they value the corporation's products and services more than its cost to produce them, the ultimate sign of market approval. Creating value has the result of profit generation.

2. **Dynamic and continuous innovation**: In their never-flagging search for satisfaction and greater value, customers utilize their power of judgment, calculation and choice as optimization tools. Their judgment is an assessment of "what's in it for me (or us)" – does the value proposition align with their felt needs and does it promise to meet them. Their calculation is comparative – what alternatives exist (including the alternative of not buying at all), and competition is always active in making alternative propositions for them to

compare. Choice is the final decision to commit to the opportunity cost of not buying the alternative. This choice environment is dynamic – preferences change, competition changes, technology advances, prices fluctuate, external shocks occur. The response from customer-led firms takes the form of innovation. They understand and empathize with the customer's continuous search for betterment, and conduct their own pursuit of new economic value that they are able to deliver as a never-ending flow of innovation. They don't think of strategy in terms of defending market share or establishing dominant power in market spaces, but in terms of how to build, expand, reinforce and extend customer delight in a world of change.

3. **Long-term horizons**: Ceaseless innovation in the pursuit of new value for customers cannot be framed in short term periodicity. It calls for continued investment in value-generating assets over extended time periods, measuring the return on those investments via metrics of customer value. Since R&D processes prior to major capital investment decisions can be uncertain both in terms of duration and outcome, firms maintain portfolios of experiments and test and projects-in-development, some of which may not come to fruition for several years. The portfolio may show as an increasing cost in corporate accounting as it develops and matures in the approach to marketplace implementation. The management of the portfolio might involve discarding or terminating a lot of experiments in the search for the most productive, customer-adopted innovations. This kind of shuffling and rebalancing and recombination of options cannot be managed with a short-term mindset. In complex systems thinking, exploration harnesses complexity by trying out large varieties over long time scales, whereas shorter term "exploitation" tends to eliminate those variations that have deficiencies before they can reach a pay-off threshold. The balance between exploration and exploitation is too tilted toward the latter in today's capitalism.

The ideology of maximizing shareholder value in the current era of financialization violates all three of the business model triad of characteristics.

• **Creating value for shareholders before customers**: The theory behind maximization of shareholder value as the guiding principle of corporate governance holds that shareholders are the only stakeholders interested in monitoring management to ensure that they allocate resources effectively (Lazonick, 2013). Shareholders are considered "residual claimants" because of their investor status. This theory of claimant status supports shareholders' receipts of dividends and the short-term appreciation of the market value of their stock certificates in preference to long-term investment in innovation. The stock appreciation sought by many of the holders of tradeable stock certificates is more influenced by short-term profits (quarterly earnings) than long-term investment in innovation for customers.

- **Reduced commitment to innovation**: Investments in innovation require a financial commitment that is in tension with the commitment to liquidity inherent in the business models of financialized corporations: consistent and predictable earnings, regular and increasing dividend payments, and short-term trading in stocks, including stock buybacks. The strategic allocation of corporate resources to uncertain innovation projects runs counter to these preferences. As William Lazonick states: Trillions of dollars that could have been spent on innovation and job creation in the US economy have instead been used to manipulate corporate stock prices. With superior performance defined as meeting Wall Street's expectations of steadily rising quarterly earnings-per-share targets, companies turned to massive stock repurchases to boost their stock prices. (Lazonick, 2013) The transition within corporations from innovation to financialization leaves them vulnerable to the decline brought on by more innovation-focused competitors.

- **Shorter-term horizons**: In 2017, McKinsey Global Institute created a Corporate Horizon Index to compare longer-term to shorter-term patterns of investment and growth among hundreds of publicly listed companies. The research concluded that short-termism was on the rise but that companies classified as long term outperformed their shorter-term peers on a range of metrics, including revenue (i.e., sales to customers), job creation, earnings and market capitalization. Firms in digital industries, such as software and biotechnology, were classified as the most long term, while firms in physical capital-based industries, such as automobiles and chemicals, were among the most short term.

Over a measurement period of 14 years (2001–2014), the revenues of long-term companies grew on average 47 percent more than those of short-term companies with far less revenue volatility. They invested almost 50 percent more annually on R&D than other companies and even increased their R&D expenditures during the 2007–8 financial crisis, while short-term companies were cutting their R&D.

In McKinsey's summary, short-termism is rising, costing millions of jobs and trillions in GDP growth (Barton, 2017, p. 2).

Evidence of the Golden Age of Corporations

The energy of customer primacy was evident in the successful corporations of the nineteenth and early twentieth centuries. Whether it was cheap illumination for homes to improve family life and family productivity, more nutritional and safer foodstuffs, sewing machines for both factories and cottage industry production, greater variety in catalogue goods, higher quality and more durable housewares or any of the production for the expanding populations and markets, the spirit of improving the lives and available choices for customers was the driver of the business model. Andrew Carnegie consistently declared his commitment to invest in new technologies and techniques, and scrap the existing ones irrespective of sunk cost, whenever there was the potential for lower costs of production and higher quality of output that he could pass on to customers.

Short-term shareholder value appreciation was not a consideration. Dividends were paid after resources were allocated for working capital and immediate investment, and capital was retained for longer-term innovation. The entrepreneurial owners were building lasting businesses on a multi-generational horizon. Managers were paid salaries for coordination and administrative services rather than incented with speculative stock market appreciation.

The Promise – and Realization – of the Digital Age

In the digital age, there is some indication of a return to these practices. In the first annual shareholder letter from Amazon (then known as amazon.com), CEO Jeff Bezos set out to establish investor expectations. The first sub-heading in the letter reads: "It's All about the Long Term." The CEO argued that creating value over the long term will result from solidifying market leadership to add power to the Amazon.com economic model and achieve stronger returns on invested capital. The metrics indicative of market leadership are customer and revenue growth, the degree to which customers purchase repeatedly, and the strength of the Amazon brand. The company's emphasis on the long term is built on an approach that emphasizes (1) relentless focus on the customer; (2) making investment decisions in light of long-term market leadership considerations rather than short-term profitability considerations or short-term Wall Street reactions; (3) making bold rather than timid investment decisions, some of which may not pay off; (4) maximizing the present value of future cash flows rather than GAAP accounting profit; (5) prioritizing growth and the need for large continuing investments to meet an expanding market opportunity.

Bezos actively sought to separate shareholders for Amazon.com, whose investment philosophy was consistent with this long-term management approach, from the pack of those more interested in short-term returns.

Professor Annika Steiber has captured the generalized potential of the new companies of the digital age to completely reimagine corporate management as an evolutionary model of continuous change (Steiber, 2014). She codifies six management principles: continuous reconfiguration of competencies, continuous change through self-organization, releasing the inherent innovation powers of creative employees, the ambidextrousness of efficient daily production and long-term innovation, an open network organization with the permeability to freely exchange information with its surroundings and partners to catalyze emergence, and a systems approach that maintains a holistic view of the economic environment. The outcome of applying these principles is more value for customers in a shorter time using the same or fewer resources, while adapting to – and proactively pushing for – the changing logic of the market.

Indeed, there is broad promise among the new crop of digital economy corporations that customer primacy has become the driver of their approach to business. In an Element in this series (Denning, 2022), Steve Denning pointed out that digital age companies with vision and mission statements dedicated to delivering benefits to customers have achieved much greater financial success than industrial age companies whose vision and mission statements are all about their performance (to be the best, to be the premier, to be the leader, etc.).

The new vision and mission statements arise from these companies' acute understanding of the role of the customer in the digitally networked economy in bringing change from the bottom up and the outside in. They have achieved this from the bottom up because individual customers have open and immediate access to unlimited information to make their choices, creating clear signals about their preferences and what works for them and what does not. Business success is no longer so much a result of top-down management decisions but bottom-up customer decisions. Digital age competitors can be faster and more competent than ever before in designing and offering new value propositions to the same customer universe. This is accomplished by interconnecting new supply chains online and developing new direct channels so customers can easily reach outside existing supplier relationships to realize new and superior benefits without significant opportunity cost.

Today – early 2024 – the promise implied in digital era vision and mission statements is fully realized in marketplace results. In June 2023, there were seven firms with a combined market capitalization of more than $10 trillion (Apple, Microsoft, Alphabet, Amazon, NVidia, Tesla, and Meta), more than a quarter of the total stock market capitalization. Since market capitalization reflects expectations of the future revenue flows these firms will receive as a result of the customer value they create, it is clear that they enjoy extraordinary customer approval as well as investor approval.

Many more firms, not limited to the technology sector, are succeeding with digital-era management: examples include Tesla in automobiles, John Deere in agricultural equipment, Domino's in fast food, Spotify in musical entertainment, and Roche and Novartis in pharmaceuticals.

There is a new and different mindset behind these digital era management models and corporate organization forms. They represent a discontinuity from the eras of financialization and command and control. Thinking in networks rather than hierarchies, and implementing via software rather than management processes, these models can accommodate, embrace, and capitalize on the new urgency of customer primacy and its dynamics of outside-in and bottom-up change and the incessant demand for continuous innovation. These new models are a realization of the reimagining of managerial capitalism as customer capitalism. The new digital-era processes and operating methods keep organizations focused on systematically achieving customer-relevant outcomes. The deep purpose of the companies employing the new models is creating value for customers, delighting them so as to secure the revenues and financial gains that enable the firm to satisfy all the other stakeholders: staff, managers, partners and shareholders, as well as society at large.

Reimagining the Economics of Capitalism

In economics, *value* is a social concept. It is conceived as a net increase in well-being. At the level of individual transactions, each party, seller and buyer, seeks to improve their situation. If they both feel better off as a result of the trade, it goes forward; if not, it does not. Scaled up to the level of the economy, economists try to capture the concept as GDP growth or Gross Output growth, recognizing that these quantitative metrics fail to fully capture the subjective value inherent in the concept of well-being. The creation of value at that level is a net plus for society. The value may not be evenly distributed, but it certainly reaches a larger constituency than shareholders, although the opposite is implied by the notion of maximizing shareholder value.

At the level of the corporation, the net increase in well-being takes place between the customer base and the employees of the firm. Once value is confirmed by customers, the value experiences of third parties such as neighbors of the factory or local communities can be taken into account, too, as far as possible. Shareholders play a different role, as holders of tradeable certificates entitling them to a share of the asset appreciation that results from the corporation's success in creating value for customers.

The importance of the employee at the interface with the customer has often been neglected in the context of the corporate focus on efficiency and financialization. Both mass production and central planning have fostered this neglect. Employee disengagement has become problematic for productivity and customer value creation.

The growth companies of the digital era combine a sensitivity to customer-centricity with an understanding of the importance of employee development and employee satisfaction in fostering a motivated, engaged, and innovative workforce. Customer-centricity does not neglect the employee; perhaps customer primacy is a better term, leaving plenty of room for focus on the role of the employee in creating value.

The process of value creation is known in economics as *entrepreneurship*. This term has lost its original meaning of undertaking the uncertain task of creating new value for customers. It has come to be associated, in the popular vernacular, with the launch of new firms and the management of small businesses. But, as the pursuit of new economic value on behalf of customers, the economic function of entrepreneurship should be the primary focus of the production side of the corporation.

We can go back to the writings of Peter Drucker to resolve the issue of entrepreneurship in large firms. He defined entrepreneurship as a management function and management responsibility (Drucker, 1993). He recognized that entrepreneurship is not limited to small or start-up businesses, and that it is a crucial discipline and practice (i.e., not a science and not an art, but the applied use of practice-derived knowledge directed toward ends) for large corporations. He linked innovation and entrepreneurship together in identifying a shift from a managerial economy to an entrepreneurial economy, built on the "new technology" (i.e., a new application of knowledge to human work) of entrepreneurial management. This new technology led to the emergence of a new kind of systematic innovation – the search for and the exploitation of new opportunities for satisfying human wants and needs. Innovation, Drucker wrote, is the specific tool of entrepreneurs, the means by which they exploit change as an opportunity. He believed it was capable of being presented as a discipline and capable of being practiced, that is, appropriate for "management."

Using McDonald's, among other cases, as illustration, he described the core practice of entrepreneurial innovation of asking "What is value to the customer?" and capturing the answer in subjective expectations of quality, predictability, speed, cleanliness, and friendliness, and designing a system that set standards for these qualitative perceptions and training and compensating human capital to meet or surpass them. Innovation, he noted, does not have to be limited to products and it's not just high tech.

Drucker located the economic concept of entrepreneurship in J. B. Say and Joseph Schumpeter, rather than in the prevailing economics of Drucker's own time, which "focuses on getting the most out of existing resources" rather than "shifting economic resources out of an area of lower and into an area of higher productivity and great yield."

Drucker wanted entrepreneurship to become the "integrating . . . .life sustaining activity in our organizations, our economy, our society." This requires, he wrote, that "executives in all institutions" make innovation and entrepreneurship a normal, ongoing, everyday activity, a practice in their own work and that of the organization. The emergence of the entrepreneurial society, he wrote in 1986, may be a major turning point in history. We must draw the conclusion that the turning point has not yet arrived. Perhaps 15 percent of the global economy is represented by the innovative, customer centric, value-creating corporations of the new digital era. But those corporations are the point of the spear of reimagining value and entrepreneurship for our century.

During the entrepreneurial ownership phase of corporate capitalism, the ownership and entrepreneurship functions were combined in one or a few individuals controlling capital and exercising entrepreneurship to create new value for customers – such as cheap and widely available illumination that extended family life in dark evenings, railroads and telegraph that opened up new, extended human relationships through transportation and communication, new safe and nutritious foods for better health and wellness, and distribution systems that connected customers and businesses on a new nationwide scale and opened up all kinds of new consumption and production possibilities.

The creativity of entrepreneurship combined with the enabling power of capital resources and technology resulted in new mass production, mass marketing, and mass distribution systems of unprecedented scale and complexity.

The entrepreneurship function therefore brought the management subfunction into being as a coordinating mechanism for the efficient operation of business at these new levels of scale. Over time, the managerial subfunction, in its search for control, repressed the entrepreneurial function. And, recently, the management function has usurped the ownership function through the channels of stock awards, stock buybacks and the ideology of maximizing shareholder value.

For capitalism to transcend the current aberrant period, it will be necessary to restore the primacy of the entrepreneurial function, exactly as Peter Drucker envisaged.

Reimagining the Relationship with Capital Markets

In June 2022, KKR, a US-based private equity firm, completed the sale of C.H.I. Overhead Doors to Nucor Corporation. KKR had purchased the company, a leading manufacturer of residential and commercial garage doors, in 2019. They saw potential for growth in market expansion, geographical expansion, innovation, and customer development. They began a number of strategic initiatives to drive growth and improve operations, including expanding product offerings, investing in new technology and automation, and optimizing the supply chain, all in the pursuit of new value that could be realized by C.H.I. customers. In 2021, C.H.I. reported record sales and profits driven by strong customer demand for its innovations and improved operational efficiency.

As part of the strategic value creation process, KKR provided equity participation to all C.H.I. Overhead Doors employees so that they all benefited from the sale of the company to its next owners. According to Business Wire (2022), all 800 employees received a payout averaging approximately $175,000.

In fact, across all of its investments as of June 2022, KKR had awarded billions of dollars of total equity value to over 45,000 non-senior employees in 25 companies in multiple sectors. KKR is a founding partner in Ownership Works, a nonprofit organization that partners with companies and investors to provide all employees with ownership via equity stakes.

KKR had once been associated with the negative reputation of private equity as "the barbarians at the gate," the corporate raiders who would devour companies at a moment of commercial weakness, load them with debt, fire employees, sell off assets, divert all available cash into dividends for themselves, and dispose of the firm quickly. The point of citing the C.H.I. Overhead Doors case is to illustrate the potential for dramatic change in the nature of the relationship between corporations and capital markets.

The problem of short-termism and the focus on maximizing shareholder value is a liability of stock markets today. They have created almost perfectly liquid, low-cost, short-term equity investments for shareholders. But companies need to engage in illiquid, high-risk, long-term investments in both physical assets and intangibles such as ideas, innovation and research and development that can take years and sometimes decades to come to fruition. While making it easier for investors to trade shares at low cost and cash in those shares on demand, we have made it harder for companies to raise patient, long term capital that does not demand that profitable cash flows be devoted to dividends and share buybacks.

But this assertion of shareholder rights has not been invariable over time and across geographies. There have been a number of structures and approaches to capital funding designed to provide corporations with the long-term perspective demanded for building both the asset base and the knowledge base for continuous innovation. One such structure is family ownership. Ford Motor Company and Mars, Inc. are familiar US-based multinationals that have historically utilized this structure. In fact, family ownership is the most common form of ownership of companies around the world.

Families are part of a more general class of shareholders sometimes called "block holders" – shareholders or groups of shareholders who own a substantial fraction of shares in a company (often defined as in excess of 25%). In most countries, three shareholders control a majority of shares in a majority of companies in a single voting block. The nature of the block holders varies across countries. In some, such as China, they are the state, but in most of Asia, Europe and South America, they are families.

Another structure for long-term focus is a dual class of shares – Google, LinkedIn, Snapchat, and Facebook all came to the stock market with dual-class structures, to allow the founders to retain and promote the purpose and values of their firms. (But dual-class share structures are not permitted in the United Kingdom.)

Historically in the United Kingdom, a shared focus on long-term corporate health was encouraged by concentrated local ownership. There were stock markets in Manchester, Birmingham, Bristol, Cardiff, Edinburgh, Glasgow, Liverpool, and Sheffield, where families entered into private financial negotiation with other notables who understood the local industry and its needs and opportunities. Over time, this ownership was diluted as stock markets centralized in London and shares were dispersed among a broader base of investors.

In Germany, until the second half of the twentieth century, banks were the custodians of family-owned shares, and cast the vote in shareholder meetings. Equity came to be owned by families and banks in complex webs of intercorporate and interbank holdings, with no transfer of control to external institutional investors or individuals. Today in Germany – and in Denmark – there are industrial foundations that own companies including Bertelsmann, Bosch, Carlsberg, Ikea, and Novo Nordisk.

In the United States, wealthy families such as Morgan, Du Pont, and Mellon controlled many business groups until the post-World War II period, but these groups have been in decline since then.

The lesson is that there are alternatives to the high liquidity, low risk equity, short-term stock trading markets of today. In fact, there has been a notable reduction in the number of publicly traded companies listed on major stock exchanges. Private equity, private debt, and other forms of alternative funding sources enable companies to raise long-term capital without going public.

In the reimagination of capital markets, the most likely future is a mixed system with less emphasis on public stock markets and more on private capital. This may take the form of private equity funds, private debt, family holdings, and trusts, or the long-term patient investment of pension funds and sovereign wealth funds. GIC, the Singaporean sovereign wealth fund, has explicitly taken a twenty-year rolling return view on investments and performance measurement. The Canada Pension Plan uses a five-year rolling return measurement as a benchmark. Long-term value creation is also the strategy of GPFG

(Norway Pension Fund), and ADIA (Abu Dhabi Investment Authority), among others. These are commitments to long-term equity ownership as against traditional short-term portfolio management.

From another angle, Hermann Simon reports from his Hidden Champions database (Simon, 2009) on a global group of 2000 companies below the visibility of large corporations, characterized by high after-tax ROI of 9.5% (versus 3.5% for the Fortune Global 500 in the comparison year of 2007) and an ROE of 24.2%, and higher than average revenue growth rates (11.6% annually for the companies in the database over $1 billion in revenue). The companies in the Hidden Champions database are characterized by high equity ratios (42% on average, and over 50% for one-third of the companies), and much of the equity is owned in large blocks by families, private equity firms and banks. These companies can take a long-term view of investing for growth and sustainability, and self-financing is the most important source of financing. Capital costs are low, and financing is not a constraint.

Whether the long-term investments in twenty-first-century capitalism are held by families, private investor blocks, private equity funds, pension funds or sovereign wealth funds, it seems reasonable to expect that the short-term trading casino activity of the major public stock markets and their denizens, including self-dealing management teams who award themselves stocks and then bid up the value of their holdings through stock buybacks, will exert less nefarious influence on investment in innovation in the future.

Reimagining Management

At a very high level, this Element has surveyed the evolution of corporate management across eras. We have identified transitions in a series of discontinuities (see Table 1) all trending toward corporate management as an internalized, top-down, hierarchical tool of authority, operating with the goal of making money for shareholders and using short term profits and current stock prices as indicators. Success is defined in terms of making the most of current businesses and resources, especially in making output targets at lower cost and higher margin. Strategy is defined as fending off competitors to build moats around the market space the company occupies.

The first service of management was as a co-ordination function for entrepreneurial owners who were creating unprecedented methods of high-speed throughput in mass production, mass distribution, and mass marketing. Management played a noble subsidiary role in bringing the visions of the entrepreneurs to life as the astounding new factories, railroads, telegraph lines, mail-order catalogs, and all their physical manifestations and supporting processes.

Table 1 The discontinuous eras of corporate capitalism.

	The discontinuous eras of corporate capitalism			
Era	**Form**	**Context**	**Customer view**	**Examples**
Pre-corporate Partnership Era	Self-funded individuals / mostly small businesses	Emerging technology applied to artisanal craft.	Increasing functional and emotional value	Wedgwood
Discontinuity: The invention of the corporation				
Era of Entrepreneurial Ownership	Entrepreneur-owned internally growth-funded large-scale corporations	Rapidly advancing industrial technology applied to mass production and distribution.	Serving expansive needs in expanding markets.	Standard Oil, Singer Sewing Machines.
Discontinuity: Entrepreneurs exit, management takes over				
Era of Managerial Capitalism	Managerially organized (e.g., M-Form) investor-funded complex organizations.	Increasing sophistication of management methods to organize production.	Increasing customer responsiveness, market segmentation.	General Motors, Procter & Gamble
Discontinuity: Control takes over				
Command and Control Era	Centralized structure of conglomerates, with central planning methods and processes.	Advances in ICT, war economy methods.	Focus on revenue efficiency, cost reduction, allocation of scarce resources under control.	GE (1950–1980), IBM
Discontinuity: Growth of Finance Sector Transforms Management				
Era of Financialization	Management via quantitative methodologies of corporate finance.	Expanding financial sector and dominance of stock markets.	Focus on maximizing shareholder value.	GE (1980 – Present)
Discontinuity: The Digital Age Redefines Management				
Dawning Digital Era	New digital forms of corporate organization based on networks not hierarchy. New production processes based on real-time automated quality controls.	Digital technologies, software, platforms, networks, rapid innovation.	Customer primacy, continuous outside-in and bottom-up improvement dynamics, self-organization.	Amazon, Microsoft

When ownership changed, management changed. In the first era of managerial capitalism, salaried innovators found new ways to serve customers better, through market segmentation, branding, and meeting emotional needs. But management's role quickly shifted to one of control, using measurement and accounting to compute new-fangled ratios illuminating the efficient use of capital, with the mindset of getting the most out of available resources. Management became the internal hierarchical power in the corporation, controlling, ordering, directing, constraining, limiting, structuring, defining, making and applying rules, and planning in such a way as to make sure the results at the end of the period were as predicted at the start of the period.

In the transition to the era of financialization, management's control focus shifted to a narrow range of financial targets, especially share price appreciation, and some subsidiary metrics including revenue growth, profits and margins, net income, earnings per share, dividends paid, and other financial ratios and analytics dictated by the stock analysts in the financial sector. Earnings reports are eagerly perused and analyzed the instant they are issued on financial sector media outlets like CNBC and Bloomberg. Real time stock prices are exhibited in common spaces in corporate offices, illustrating the intense and unrelenting attention to financial metrics.

Happily, we believe that the current discontinuity of the new digital era will result in a shift to a different and better direction. Top-down internal control mechanisms will be superseded by change that comes from the outside in and the bottom up. This pattern of change is characteristic of complex systems where outcomes are emergent rather than predictable, cause and effect are not clear, and control is unachievable. How can management operate in such an environment?

One example that is beginning to show real promise for success in this new management comes from Tesla and SpaceX, companies led by Elon Musk, who advocates his own forms of entrepreneurial management, including elements such as (Denning, 2023):

- Extremely flat organization, with structural hierarchy and bureaucracy eliminated as much as possible and replaced with situational leadership.
- Most work is accomplished in cross-functional teams, flexibly deployed so that individuals can leave and join freely, based on the needs of the team and the task at hand for specialized expertise. There are no job descriptions to limit the potential contribution of individuals.
- High-speed development cycles (called "sprints") such that multiple hardware changes can be made on a car model every day and every week – no more "model years."

- Continuous automated rapid testing – every car and every rocket "puts itself through" comprehensive automated compliance and certification testing.
- Short-term problem-solving over long-term planning. According to one insider, "VW makes a nine-year financial plan; Tesla doesn't know what it will be doing in 9 years but focuses on solving problems in 20 minutes or less."
- Budget allocations can be made in seconds or minutes via software without the need for formal reviews. In fact, traditional budgeting is eliminated and replaced by rolling, real-time algorithmic allocation of resources to their highest value uses.
- Most middle management is eliminated and replaced by A.I. to provide real time information about the implication of employee actions for the corporation's mission and goal.
- People are motivated to self-improve. Digital self-management provides real-time feedback without managerial monitoring. There are no annual personnel reviews.

No doubt there are imperfections in the Tesla/SpaceX implementation of digital-age management, yet it undoubtedly points to the accelerated success of the new breed of digital-era leaders like Elon Musk. The newly reimagined pattern of management exhibits these characteristics:

Principles Not Rules

To date, management has traditionally relied on rules, administrative methods, linear processes, job descriptions, plans, deliverables, and the tools of internal control. These are no longer applicable amidst the rapid exogenous change that typifies the digital era. The alternative to rules-based management is principles-based management: management that recognizes, embraces and applies customer primacy, management that lets customers initiate and drive processes, management that removes all obstacles to the realization of the very best customer experience. Management becomes more discovery than determinate, more humble than hubristic, more uncertain than predictive.

Purpose

The primary principle for the new management is clarity of the purpose of the corporation, unambiguously stated and embraced and believed by all involved. The corporate purpose is always some distinctive and differentiated variant of obsession with creating a superior value experience for customers. The most successful companies work hard upon design and articulation of the purpose statement and the purpose culture.

The Customer Is the Business Model

Shared purpose of this kind results in new management understanding of the business model. When the purpose of the company is delivering a delightful customer value experience, the customer becomes the business model. The components are knowing and understanding the customer and their wants, needs and preferences, and designing and delivering a value proposition to meet those needs and match those preferences, with responsiveness to feedback loops that come directly from customers. The customer is the entirety of the business model.

The leading companies of the digital era are implementing the model. Amazon has expressed it as "working backwards from the customer." Microsoft captures the model in its mission of "helping people and businesses throughout the world realize their full potential" – since only those people and businesses can know their own potential, they are driving the Microsoft business model.

Subjective Value and Empathy

The determination of value in this new model lies entirely with the customer. Value is subjective – determined by the customer's feelings and identified in their mental evaluation. Therefore, a core skill for the corporation is empathy, the ability to diagnose customer feelings, how they make choices, and how they develop the mental models that determine those choices. Empathy is not a process that can be mapped or automated but a cultural orientation that can be nurtured. The more empathic company succeeds.

Revenue Growth and Profit are Emergent Outcomes

Instead of specifying exact revenue and profit targets, modern management recognizes these variables as outcomes of the customer-first business model. Cash flow becomes the primary indicator, since revenues are entirely determined by the customer's willingness to buy which reflects the empathic accuracy and design of the value proposition. Companies can choose the costs that best align with cash flow generation, defining margin and profit as trailing rather than leading indicators.

Leadership Is Distributed, and Flow Replaces Hierarchy

Leadership is a management concept that has been very profitable for the business schools that teach it and the publishers of business books whose authors write about it. Its actual value in management contexts is not always clear, and it's generally identified after the fact. Leading companies are said to have great leadership at the top.

In the new management era, leadership is a role that is available to all members of the corporation. It's situational and contextual. The individual with the most appropriate and relevant knowledge, experience and expertise in a specific situation is called upon to use that expertise on behalf of a peer group or a team that is applying shared values and collaborative effort to achieve an agreed-upon end. Leadership is action rather than influence. It's not only located at the top of the firm, and it's not authority. As with many other aspects of the customer-first business, leadership is decentralized and highly distributed. Guided autonomy for those in direct contact with customers and markets is replacing middle management and its controlling rules.

Subjective Value Requires Subjective Calculation

Management has been locked into the positivist tradition that everything can be objectively and numerically measured, and that mathematics is the most important business language: the language of numbers, charts, trends, targets, share prices. Value is a number in this tradition, and so value creation must be open to mathematical analysis.

But in the customer primacy model where value is subjective and empathy is the core business skill, numerical analysis cannot be granted the dominant role in managerial calculation. The accounting discipline, which translates every action into numbers, cannot be the only source of management truth.

Management theorists Peter Lewin and Nicolas Cachanosky have, in fact, introduced the concept of subjective calculation for business (Lewin & Cachanosky, 2019). They combine the entrepreneurial management approach advocated by Peter Drucker with the notion that capital is value – value experienced by the customer as a result of the flow of services enabled by entrepreneurially assembled capital. Subjective calculation is executed in the entrepreneurial spirit by first identifying the subjective value that it's possible to create in the future (a qualitative estimation), transposing that qualitative estimate into a potential revenue and cash flow (quantitative), designing (qualitatively) and estimating (quantitatively) the cost of assembling. In this way, subjectivism and numeracy are combined in subjective calculation.

9 Conclusion

The beginnings of the remarkable rise in human well-being driven by capitalism precede the introduction of the corporation to the system, but it was the energy of the corporation that extended, accelerated, and reinforced that rise. Today's corporations bring us a cornucopia of accessible knowledge, an abundant supply of products and services of all kinds, an advanced infrastructure of communications and computing, and virtually unlimited transportation and mobility. The corporation is a brilliant invention of capitalism to deliver these outcomes; the primary protagonist of our economic system has served its customers well.

While we owe these benefits to the corporation, the entropy in the system of corporate capitalism threatens the very customer value that we expect the corporation to generate. What we refer to in Section 7 as financialization, bureaucratization, the failures of management science, the destructive entanglement of corporations with government, the uselessness of prevailing economics, and the distorted purpose of the corporation all point in a negative direction.

The promise of the digital age is to reverse this direction. There is a new dynamic in motion that points to the potential for a return to the golden age of corporations, where owner-entrepreneurs harnessed new technology for the good of customers, bending the curve of prosperity and well-being into a steeper ascent.

• A new system of value creation is evolving. Value is defined as an experience that customers desire or aspire to, and innovation and delivery are driven directly by customer behaviors and customer preferences. The nineteenth-century golden age system of value creation was based on mass production and mass distribution to take the new benefits of applied technologies such as affordable illumination, electric power, telecommunications, chemicals, steel, railroads, nutritious and affordable packed foods, catalog marketing, sewing machines, and eventually automobiles to every city street, every factory, town, village and household. The direction of motion was from the producer to the customer, with a delayed feedback loop to signal satisfaction or dissatisfaction.

The direction of motion in the new system is from the customer directly to the corporation, via networks and software, permitting a more direct influence of customer preferences on resource allocation and management practices. Digital technology requires multi-directional customer monitoring and deep customer understanding, and translation of customer data into design and implementation of strategy that creates value for customers first and, as a subsequent result, for all other stakeholders. Given the speed of change – both in technology and customer behaviors and preferences – corporate strategy needs to be agile and forward looking, with no time to stop and lock in "best practices" or "competitive advantage." The best practice is customer understanding and the competitive advantage is customer empathy. The new system promises a return to the principles of customer sovereignty.

- In the digital age, corporations can no longer be fortresses, defining and defending boundaries to establish dominant positions in markets or industries. They must compete on customer satisfaction and customer service with new corporations that come at them from all directions. Business school professors used to call this the danger of disruption (a defensive concept) while today they refer to the quick generation of software updates that make user experiences better, the rapid exploration of new product and service possibilities, and speedy abandonment of ideas that prove unsuccessful as a result of low customer acceptance. The faster pace of technological change decreases the amount of time corporations have to adapt. Corporate management is committing to fast-paced, continuous renewal, embracing the implications for corporate structure (more network than hierarchy), processes (less formal), planning (more responsive than prescriptive), and command and control style (no longer viable).
- Similarly, there will be a net disentanglement of business from government, as a result of a growing realization that the potential for corporations to improve customers' lives at an increasing pace through digital innovation is hampered by encumbering regulations that are slow to change. Throughout this Element, we have noted selected instances of entanglement that have resulted in or exacerbated developments that subtract from customer value. SEC Rule 10b-18 encourages the diversion of earnings from reinvestment in customer value to distribution to other claimants. The carried interest rules for taxing private equity returns encourage the tilting of PE financial engineering to favor fund partners and investors rather than customer communities. Complicated corporate taxation and other forms of regulation spawn the development and expansion of huge bureaucracies within both the government and the corporation, on the one side for control and on the other for compliance, both of which are obstacles to customer service and innovation.
- While it is clearly the case that much of the entanglement we observe is encouraged by both parties to it, it is likely that the pace of progress in the customer value driven digital corporation will reach an escape velocity that leaves behind the desire for regulatory protections. This is a necessary development for both the realization of the full potential of the capitalist system and for the restoration of trust.
- The digital age also catalyzes a new relationship between the corporation and its employees, the suppliers of labor (both physical and cognitive) still required at our current state of development. Software developers provide the labor that is the very heart of today's corporate production system, and they are redefining the concept of productivity. Productivity metrics are one of the central ideas of quantitative analytical economics: the mathematical ratio of outputs to inputs.

But just as the software world generated a new concept of management – "agile" – it is replacing mathematical thinking about productivity with a much more subjective, qualitative and nuanced approach that places human values above the algebraic calculation of output-to-input ratios. Some productivity researchers sum up this emerging approach in the aphorism that productivity for a software developer is "having a good day." A good day is defined both qualitatively and quantitatively in a measurement process with the acronym SPACE:

○ S: satisfaction and well-being – how fulfilled, happy and healthy one feels.
○ P: performance – an outcome of a process.
○ A: activity – the count of actions or outputs.
○ C: communication and collaboration – how people talk and work together.
○ E: efficiency and flow – doing work with minimal delays or interruptions.

The SPACE system of productivity measurement is being explored at Microsoft and several more members of IEEE, the world's largest technical professional organization. The promising signal is that, in the engine room of the modern digital corporation, where code is written, there is a move away from the purely mathematical analysis of production to a blended assessment that combines well-being, action and performance. Just as the principles of agile software development migrated to the executive suite and management ranks in business, so the principles of SPACE can migrate to how corporations judge their own production, placing more emphasis on the satisfaction and well-being of customers, whilst also encompassing the same concerns of employees.

The implication is that profit will be seen as an outcome of this focus, not a purpose in itself. Collaboration with suppliers and institutions in pursuit of satisfaction for customers will be elevated over competition versus rival businesses for market share. In order to achieve flow, management teams will be encouraged in the removal of obstacles such as bureaucracy, rigid or over-specified processes, excess government entanglement and anti-productive regulation, and excessive deference to the demands of the financial sector.

A term that is emerging to capture this new reality is *entrepreneurial management*. Management, in this construct, is not only the operational role of planning, budgeting, controlling and achieving technical efficiency but also, and more importantly, the creative and intuitive role of sensing new and changing but still latent customer needs, shaping the value creation opportunity they represent, designing new business models for new value propositions, and investing in the new capital combinations required for delivery. The uncertainty and unpredictability inherent in these activities do not align with command-and-control structures, highly specified process maps, precise numerical planning, and reliable and consistently managed earnings.

The concept of entrepreneurial management can combine the values of the entrepreneurial ownership that characterized the first large-scale corporations – the harnessing of technology by entrepreneurial owners to improve the well-being of every customer and thereby achieve new levels of quality of economic life – with the new vision of the digital age that couldn't be contemplated back then, including better healthcare for all, greater access to better and better education, availability of knowledge to all, more empathic services and a growing economy. The promise illustrated by the exponential growth of GDP per capita in the chart at the beginning of this Element can be extended. The corporation will continue to be the primary protagonist, unburdened of the pressures of financialization and the dragging anchor of bureaucracy. With this reimagining, there is the potential to return to a high standard of customer capitalism.

Epilogue: Aberrant Capitalism

The promise of the digital era is to lead us out of a period of aberrant capitalism. The great nineteenth-century surge in value creation and consumer well-being resulted from a form of capitalism characterized by entrepreneurial ownership. Visionary individuals, founder groups, and families built thriving corporations to serve flourishing, growing nations, harnessing the astonishing technological innovations of their time.

In that age of unprecedented innovation and expansion, the entrepreneurial spirit ignited a revolution of managerial systems that had the capability to orchestrate operations of staggering magnitude. But with the stepping back of the original entrepreneurs, the very bones of the corporate structures they had built began to warp and decay. A quartet of insidious forces began to eat away at the foundations of our capitalist system:

- The outdated notions of command-and-control management born in the 1940s.
- The centralized planning models that held sway through the 1950s and 1960s.
- The misguided ambitions of maximizing shareholder value that became gospel in the 1970s.
- The surge of financialization that began to control the narrative in the 1990s.

These elements have come together to create a devastatingly destructive entropy, a perversion of capitalism into a caricature of itself that, if left unchecked, threatens to obliterate the far-reaching benefits to human welfare that genuine capitalism can deliver. These corrosive forces have their roots in the very institution that once stood as the beacon of capitalism's success: the corporation, with its systems of management, methods, and missions. The economic players and institutions that propagate these forces are wreaking havoc on capitalism, not merely in its ability to elevate every participant, but in its fundamental ethos: to produce for others as an act of service, with profit as a by-product rather than a driving objective.

As a result, capitalism's reputation has been tarnished and its true purpose distorted. The consequences are dire: a widening chasm of inequality, disillusionment, and distrust, and the empowerment of those who would see the entire system dismantled. This twisted form of capitalism stands as a stark warning of the dangers that arise when we allow the forces of centralization, financialization, and the shortsighted pursuit of shareholder value to dictate the course of our economic system.

In the face of such unrelenting entropy, it is our responsibility as the inheritors of capitalism's promise to reassert the values that underpin this system: the power of free markets to drive innovation, the potential of business to uplift societies, and the inherent dignity of labor. Only by acknowledging these threats and working tirelessly to counteract their effects, can we reclaim the true spirit of capitalism and ensure a more equitable, prosperous future for all.

References

Addicott, D. A. (2017). The rise and fall of the Zaibatsu: Japan's industrial and economic modernization. *Global Tides*, **11**(1), 5.

Advertising Age. (1988). *Procter and Gamble: The House that Ivory Built*. Lincolnwood, IL: NTC Business Books.

Arthur, W. B. (2023). Economics in Nouns and Verbs. *Journal of Economic Behavior and Organization*.

Arthur, W. B. (2009). *The Nature of Technology: What it is and How it Evolves*, New York: Free Press.

Barton, D., Manyika, J., Koller, T., et al. (2017). Measuring the impact of short termism. *McKinsey Quarterly*, 57–63.

Birnbaum, J. H. (1993). *The Lobbyists*, New York: Times Books.

Blackford, M. G. (n.d.). *The Rise of the Corporate Economy*.

Burton W. F., Jr. (2013). *The Myth of the Robber Barons*, Herndon, VA: Young America's Foundation.

Business Wire. (2022). KKR Completes Sale Of C.H.I. Overhead Doors. *Business Wire*.

Cantillon, R. (2010). *An Essay on Economic Theory*, Auburn, AL: Ludwig von Mises Institute.

Carnegie, A. (1906). Gospel of Wealth II. *North American Review*, 183(604), 1096–1106.

Catton, B. (1969). *War Lords Of Washington*, Westport, CT: Greenwood Press.

Chandler, A. D. (1977). *The Visible Hand: The Managerial Revolution in American Business*, Cambridge, MA: Harvard University Press.

Clark, G. (2007). *A Farewell to Alms: A Brief Economic History of the World*, Princeton: Princeton University Press.

Clark, J. B. (1899). *The Distribution of Wealth*, New York: Macmillan.

Cohan, W. D. (2022). *Power Failure: The Rise and Fall of an American Icon*, New York: Penguin Random House.

Cohen, M. D., & Axelrod, R. (2000). *Harnessing Complexity: Organizational Implications of a Scientific Frontier*, New York: Basic Books.

Cortada, J. W. (2019). *IBM: The Rise and Fall and Reinvention of a Global Icon*, Cambridge, MA: MIT Press.

Corwin, E. (1947). *Total War and the Constitution*, New York: Knopf.

Crews, C. W. (2021). Competitive Enterprise Institute. June 30. Accessed January 26, 2023. Cei.org.

Denning, S. (2022). *Reinventing Capitalism in The Digital Age*, Cambridge: Cambridge University Press.

Denning, S. (2023). How World Domination Is Within Tesla's Grasp. *Forbes*, June 12, www.forbes.com/sites/stevedenning/2023/06/12/how-world-domination-is-within-teslas-grasp/?sh=6fb947637490 (Accessed July 14, 2023).

Di Lorenzo, T. J. (1985). The origins of anti-trust: An interest-group perspective. *International Review of Law and Economics*, **5**(1), 73–88.

Drucker, P. (1993). *Innovation and Entrepreneurship: Practice and Principles*, New York: Harper Collins.

Dyer, D., Dalzell, F., & Olegario, R. (2004). *Rising Tide: Lessons from 165 Years of Brand Building at Procter and Gamble*, Boston, MA: Harvard Business School Press.

Feldman, M., & Kenney, M. (2023). *Private Equity and the Demise of the Local: The Loss of Community Economic Power and Autonomy*. Cambridge: Cambridge University Press (2024).

Fishlow, A. (1966). Productivity and technological change in the railroad sector, 1840–1910. In *Output, Employment, and Productivity in the United States after 1800* edited by A. Fishlow, Washington DC: National Bureau of Economic Research, pp. 583–646. www.nber.org/books-and-chapters/output-employment-and-productivity-united-states-after-1800/productivity-and-technological-change-railroad-sector-1840-1910 (Accessed July 14, 2023).

Fruin, W. M. (1992). *The Japanese Enterprise System: Competitive Strategies and Cooperative Structures*. Oxford: Oxford University Press.

Graeber, D. (2019). *Bullshit Jobs: A Theory*, New York: Simon and Schuster.

Gregg, S. (2022). *The Next American Economy*, New York: Encounter Books.

Gulati, R. (2022). *Deep Purpose: The Heart and Soul of High Performance Companies*, New York, NY: Harper Collins.

Halbertsam, D. (1986.) *The Reckoning*, New York: William Morrow.

Hamel, G., & Zanini, M. (2017). What we learned about bureaucracy from 7,000 HBR readers. *Harvard Business Review*.

Hawley, E. W. (1966). *The New Deal and the Problem of Monopoly*, Princeton: Princeton University Press.

Higgs, R. (1987). *Crisis and Leviathan*, Oxford: Oxford University Press.

Jeuck, B. E., & John E. (1950). *Catalogues and Counters*, Chicago, IL: University Of Chicago Press.

Johnson, P. (2001). The prospering fathers. In *Colossus: How The Corporation Changed America*, edited by J. Beatty, New York: Broadway Books, pp. 2869–3035.

Jones, J. H. (1951). *Fifty Billion Dollars: My Thirteen Years with the RFC*, New York: Macmillan.

Klein, M. (1993). *The Flowering of the Third America*, Chicago, IL: Ivan R. Dee.

Knight, F. H. (1982). *Freedom and Reform: Essays in Economics and Social Philosophy*, Indianapolis: Liberty Press.

Kristol, I. (1995). *Adam Smith and the Spirit of Capitalism*, London: Free Press.

Lazonick, W. (2013). From innovation to financialization: How shareholder value ideology is destroying the US economy. In *The Handbook of the Political Economy of Financial Crises*, edited by G. and Wolfson, M. H. Epstein. Oxford: Oxford University Press.

Lazonick, W. (2010). Innovative business models and varieties of capitalism: Financialization of the US corporation. *Business History Review*, **1**, 675–702.

Legerbott, S. (1966). United states transport advance and externalities. *Journal of Economic History*, **26**(4), 444–446.

Levy, J. (2021). *Ages of American Capitalism*, New York: Random House.

Lewin, P., & Cachanosky, N. (2019). *Austrian Capital Theory*, Cambridge: Cambridge University Press.

Liefmann, R. (1910). *Cartels and Trusts and the Further Development of Economic Organisation*, Routledge: Library of Jurisprudence and Political Science.

Marquette, A. F. (1967). *Brands, Trademarks and Goodwill*, New York: Mcgraw Hill.

McCraw, T. K. (1997). *Creating Modern Capitalism: How Entrepreneurs, Companies, and Countries Triumphed in Three Industrial Revolutions*, Cambridge, MA: Harvard University Press.

McCraw, T. K., & William R. C. (2018). *American Business Since 1920: How it Worked*, Hoboken, NJ: Wiley.

McGee, J. S. (1958). Predatory price cutting: The standard oil (N.J.) case. *The Journal of Law and Economics*, **1**, 137–169.

Openstax, Contributing. (2022). *US history: Political corruption in postbellum America*, Houston, TX: Rice.edu.

Persch, C. (2020). What Exactly Is Entropy? Cantor's Paradise. www.cantorsparadise.com/what-exactly-is-entropy-2a0e2fc067f8.

Perez, C. (2002). *Technological Revolutions and Financial Capital*, Cheltenham: Edward Elgar.

Philippon, T. (2019). *The Great Reversal: How America Gave up on Free Markets*, Cambridge, MA: Harvard University Press.

Rona, P. (2017). Ethics, Economics and The Corporation. In *Economics As A Moral Science*, edited by Peter and Zsolnai, Laszlo Rona, 199–249. Cham, Switzerland: Springer.

Rosenzweig, P. (2017). *The Halo Effect and the Eight Other Delusions that Deceive Managers*, New York: Free Press.

Rothbard, M. N. (2017). *The Progressive Era*, Auburn, AL: Mises Institute.

Schiff. M., & Lewin, A. Y. (1970). The impact of people on budgets, *The Accounting Review*, **45**(2), 259–268.

Schiff. M., & Lewin A. Y. (1974). *Behavioral Aspects of Accounting*, Upper Saddle River, NJ: Prentice-Hall.

Schumpeter, J. A. (1950a). Papers and Proceedings of the 62nd Annual Meeting of the AEA. *The American Economic Review (American Economic Association)*, **133**, 446–456.

Schumpeter, J. P. (1950b). *Capitalism, Socialism and Democracy*, New York: Harper & Row.

Simon, H. (2009). *Hidden Champions of the Twenty-First Century*, New York: Springer.

Steiber, A. (2014). *The Google Model: Managing Continuous Innovation in a Changing World*, Heidelberg: Springer.

Tedlow, R. S. (1991). *The Rise of the American Business Corporation* (Vol. 48). Philadelphia: Psychology Press.

Teece, D. J. (2016). Dynamic capabilities and entrepreneurial management in large organizations: Toward a theory of the (entrepreneurial) firm. *European Economic Review*, **86**, 202–216.

Tilly, R. H. (1986). German banking, 1850–1914: Development assistance for the strong. *Journal of European Economic History*, **15**(1), 113.

Von Mises, L. (1944). *Bureaucracy*, Yale: Yale University Press.

Wardley, S. (2020). *Wardley Mapping*, London: GCATI.

Wiebe, R. H. (1967). *The Search for Order*, New York: Farrar, Strauss and Giroux.

Williamson, O. E. (1963). Managerial discretion and business behavior. *The American Economic Review*, **53**(5), 1032–1057.

Williamson, O. E. (1970). *Corporate Control and Business Behavior*, Prentice Hall.

Cambridge Elements ☰

Reinventing Capitalism

Arie Y. Lewin

Duke University

Arie Y. Lewin is Professor Emeritus of Strategy and International Business at Duke University, Fuqua School of Business. He is an Elected Fellow of the Academy of International Business and a Recipient of the Academy of Management inaugural Joanne Martin Trailblazer Award. Previously, he was Editor-in-Chief of *Management and Organization Review* (2015–2021) and the *Journal of International Business Studies* (2000–2007), founding Editor-in-Chief of *Organization Science* (1989–2007), and Convener of Organization Science Winter Conference (1990–2012). His research centers on studies of organizations' adaptation as co-evolutionary systems, the emergence of new organizational forms, and adaptive capabilities of innovating and imitating organizations. His current research focuses on de-globalization and decoupling, the Fourth Industrial Revolution, and the renewal of capitalism.

Till Talaulicar

University of Erfurt

Till Talaulicar holds the Chair of Organization and Management at the University of Erfurt where he is also the Dean of the Faculty of Economics, Law and Social Sciences. His main research expertise is in the areas of corporate governance and the responsibilities of the corporate sector in modern societies. Professor Talaulicar is Editor-in-Chief of Corporate Governance: An International Review, Senior Editor of Management and Organization Review and serves on the Editorial Board of Organization Science. Moreover, he has been Founding Member and Chairperson of the Board of the International Corporate Governance Society (2014–2020).

About the Series

This series seeks to feature explorations about the crisis of legitimacy facing capitalism today, including the increasing income and wealth gap, the decline of the middle class, threats to employment due to globalization and digitalization, undermined trust in institutions, discrimination against minorities, global poverty and pollution. Being grounded in a business and management perspective, the series incorporates contributions from multiple disciplines on the causes of the current crisis and potential solutions to renew capitalism.

Panmure House is the final and only remaining home of Adam Smith, Scottish philosopher and 'Father of modern economics.' Smith occupied the House between 1778 and 1790, during which time he completed the final editions of his master works: The Theory of Moral Sentiments and The Wealth of Nations. Other great luminaries and thinkers of the Scottish Enlightenment visited Smith regularly at the House across this period. Their mission is to provide a world-class twenty-first-century centre for social and economic debate and research, convening in the name of Adam Smith to effect positive change and forge global, future-focussed networks.

ADAM SMITH
PANMURE
HOUSE

Cambridge Elements $\equiv$

Reinventing Capitalism

Made in the USA
Las Vegas, NV
14 March 2024

87189371R00055